Sandy and Sandy

A
Tail of L♥ve

Sandy and Sandy

A

Tail of L♥ve

By

Sandy Spiwak-Wallin

Unedited

authorHOUSE®

AuthorHouse™
1663 Liberty Drive
Bloomington, IN 47403
www.authorhouse.com
Phone: 1-800-839-8640

Published by AuthorHouse   10/05/2012

ISBN:978-1-4772-6096-8 (sc)
ISBN: 978-1-4772-6097-5 (e)

Library of Congress Control Number: 2012912205

Any people depicted in stock imagery provided by Thinkstock are models, and such images are being used for illustrative purposes only. Certain stock imagery © Thinkstock.

This book is printed on acid-free paper.

Dedication

Dedicated in loving memory of Barton Simon whose dog Sandy is loved and cared for beyond his wildest dreams and expectations.

And for Sandy, my beloved canine child and love of my life, my best friend, confidante, soul mate, philosopher, muse and bon vivant.

And for my husband Fred Wallin, for being a good sport.

And for my mother Fortuna and brother Randy Spiwak, for always being there for me.

And for all the homeless, neglected and abused animals out there in the world, may the angels watch over you.

Acknowledgments

A big "thank you" to my wonderful neighbor Warren Harrell, for his invaluable help with my computer.

And to Lori Golden, Publisher-Editor of The Pet Press, for being the first to publish my articles and allowing my voice to be heard.

Chapters

Chapter One

FAREWELL BARTON

When Barton, my husband's cousin died suddenly of skin cancer, he left behind "Sandy," a five year old unsocialized Sheltie. Fred and I had promised him that we would take Sandy in and care for her, as he had no other family to rely upon. At the time we could not have imagined how this little creature would completely turn our world upside down and also be responsible for enriching our lives, bringing us love and joy, and completing us as human beings in the coming years.

In the weeks preceding Barton's death we were busy taking him to chemotherapy, and helped with grocery shopping, banking, lawyers, and sadly also helped him plan his own funeral arrangements. From the time of his grim diagnosis, melanoma had spread throughout his body like wildfire and I was shocked at how quickly he was deteriorating.

We had very little time to discuss his beloved Sheltie's history, but we knew that Sandy was very timid, distrustful, high-strung, and very sheltered.

The former surfer boy was a bit of a loner who preferred to go out rather than having people come over, and Sandy had practically no contact with the outside world.

The first time I met Barton was the day his mother, Sally, died. Fred and I went over to pay our respects and to visit with him and that is when I first met Sandy. I thought she was the prettiest little girl I had ever seen with her beautiful doe eyes and her silky sable and white fur. With delicate and refined features, and very feminine, she reminded me of Bambi. When I asked Barton what his dog's name was he said, "you guys have the same name." Who would have believed that Barton would die three years later and that we would become unsuspecting parents to Sandy, our future canine child?

Fred and Barton had not stayed in touch as much as they had during their childhood though they were still very close and Aunt Sally's death brought them even closer together. Barton became an extended member of our family and was always included in all of our family gatherings especially during Thanksgiving at my mother's house.

Fred and I did not have an occasion to go over to Barton's house again until he became ill, and had to stay in the hospital overnight after some tests. He had asked us to go over to his house to feed Sandy that night, and when we got there it was pitch black. Sandy was completely petrified especially when we entered her home without Barton. She had never spent the night alone and didn't know where he was.

She barked and barked at us, and as we made our way into the kitchen, she quickly ran inside her bedroom where all her toys were and sat beside her bed, her safe spot. She was trembling uncontrollably and so afraid of us. She thought we were total strangers who had invaded her home and were going to hurt her. I guess three years later she would not have remembered our scent from the one time that we first met and she was not used to having people come over to her house.

It was already eight o'clock and she must have been starving; yet Sandy refused to eat her dinner. I called her to the kitchen several times but she did not respond and then decided to take her food to her room, but she still would not eat.

I sat on the carpet and tried petting her and spoke softly to her, but she would just look away not making eye contact, still trembling and not dealing with us, pretending we were not there. Sandy has such a vulnerable quality that makes you want to just hug her forever.

I told Fred to also sit down with us and to try petting her while I got some biscuits from the pantry. Sandy still would not accept anything from our hands, so I put some treats on the ground hoping that would do the trick. We just kept on talking to her gently and when the trembling subsided about an hour later, Sandy finally and with a lot of hesitation, shyly took a biscuit from the palm of my hand. It was right then and there that I fell in love with her and felt a deep connection between us. When I got up, she followed me to the kitchen and finally ate her dinner. I had never seen a dog eat so fast. We had finally bonded.

Before we left for the night, I turned the TV on very low so that she would feel comforted by the sound of voices and I left some soft lighting throughout the house so she wouldn't be scared since it was going to be Sandy's first night alone.

When Fred picked up Barton from the hospital the following afternoon, he called me up at work to relay what the doctor had told him. Barton would not live beyond the year.

At first I did not believe Fred since he has a tendency to be a bit of a hypochondriac, and exaggerate the medical facts. But a couple of weeks later when I saw Barton again, I could not believe how frail he had become. I knew then that it wouldn't be long before he would be leaving us.

Barton was undergoing chemotherapy, and was not responding well to the treatments and after a while decided that it was futile, that it just making him more ill, and that he would instead" just ride it out like a wave in the ocean."

Between Fred, Maryanne, his long time family friend, my mom, my brother and I, we tried our best to comfort him on a daily basis but it wasn't enough, and we kept on insisting that he needed live in care.

Barton fought us on that topic for about a month, until I informed him that I would be bringing Berta in to stay with him Monday through Friday, and that we would alternate between all of us over the weekends. At that point he was too weak to argue with me because he knew that I was right.

When I first met Berta, she was taking care of my mother's 100-year old uncle Victor, who lived in a high rise in Brentwood. He was very healthy, alert and independent, and didn't particularly care for Berta because she was "bossy and too old"(she was 65). He himself was very overbearing and was becoming increasingly cantankerous, and there was no room for two alpha-dogs living under the same roof. I sure hope I don't live that long because I will be absolutely impossible! Uncle Victor ended up living to 104 years of age.

At the time we were faced with the same dilemma most of us have to face sooner or later in our lives. "Who will take care of our aging parents, siblings, other relatives or in-laws?" Fred's mother, Bernice had suffered a stroke and it changed the family dynamic instantly. Fred's other brothers took Bernice along with Jack, their dad, to a nursing home, because even though Jack was mentally alert he was not capable of taking care of himself and needed help with bathing and dressing among other things. However, Fred and I felt that Jack had no business being in a nursing home, because as long as he had live-in-help in his own home, he would be alright and much more happy and comfortable in his familiar surroundings with his personal belongings. So when I heard that Berta had left Uncle Victor I was thrilled!

I offered her a job and she quickly accepted. I knew Berta would be perfect for Jack, who loved being spoiled. Berta, who liked to be in charge, was also happy to live away from her children. And for the next five years that she cared for Jack, she would only visit them and her grandchildren on the weekends, and sometimes chose to stay in. Berta herself had a newfound sense of freedom. She had her own big room and bathroom and cable TV. Just like Barton though, at first Jack resisted us saying, "Berta doesn't speak English, I can't understand a word she says, and she won't know how to do my diabetic test." I responded with "that is why we are going to practice right now."

Anybody who has ever taken care of the ill or elderly soon finds out that it can take a toll on your wellbeing and sometimes it depletes the life out of you. And then the question becomes, "who takes care of the caregiver?"

At the same time I had also made arrangements to bring in Luis, a foreign exchange student from Spain, who was getting his masters in computer game design. He needed a place to live and would be going to school most of the time, so all we needed was for him to watch Jack and keep him company over the weekends as a condition. Luis would also take him out for drives during breakfast, lunch and dinner since he didn't cook. This made things more exciting for Jack, because Luis was anxious to explore the city, and especially because Jack was allowed to go off his diabetic diet with moderation. Once in a while Jack could eat a cheeseburger or pie if he felt like it, which was always the case since he had a great appetite.

My theory about old people with illnesses is that their cause of death is rarely due to their illness, since they are so overly medicated in order to extend their lives. In my opinion the biggest disease in the world, especially for old people, is loneliness. And as far as I am concerned, it is an epidemic.

Jack's new living arrangement became a win-win situation for all of us, and with Berta he was able to visit Bernice at the nursing home on a daily basis with the help of Access Transportation, which specializes in the disabled or the elderly. Jack now also had Luis to watch all the sports games and movies with on TV. It is amazing how quickly Jack, all of the sudden, understood everything that Berta said, once she started cooking for him. I suppose the language of food is universal.

Fred and I were also relieved with this new living arrangement because quite frankly, we were exhausted from making the twice weekly, one hour-each-way, treks to the other side of town to visit Jack and then have to also grocery shop for yet another hour. I'll never forget the day that it took us 3 hours to see him because of a bad traffic accident.

We had brought Jack bagfuls of groceries when suddenly he stormed out of the kitchen. When I asked him what was wrong, Jack answered, "You forgot the grapefruit!" I realized that that in itself, was a cardinal sin, and I didn't want to continue to see Jack sulking so I went back to the store and got him a weeks' supply while Fred kept him company.

Barton had become ill shortly after Bernice's and Jack's death and we needed Berta to help us out again.

Once Berta arrived, she didn't want to leave Barton alone overnight, and refused to go home for the weekends even though she desperately needed some rest. She was a very devoted, caring, and compassionate caretaker. Berta had lost a young son to stomach cancer, and she felt it was her duty to care for Barton round the clock. She understood his pain.

Barton was secretly thrilled to have her around to help care for him and Sandy. Having someone there especially to keep him company provided comfort and made his pain, both physical and emotional, as well as his loneliness more bearable. Sandy, who does not warm up to strangers too well, surprisingly liked Berta right away, and would often steal personal items from her. Maybe Berta reminded her of Aunt Sally. Barton was too proud to admit that he needed Berta but showed his appreciation by doubling her salary after only one week.

It made me sad that Barton had never married because I am convinced that he would still be alive today. Men who are married or who live with someone take better care of themselves and will get more frequent medical check-ups at the insistence of their partners.

If melanoma is detected in its very early stages, it doesn't have to be a death sentence.

I once asked Barton why he was still single, especially since he had good looks and a funny personality with a sardonic sense of humor, and he said that it was just easier to go out and have a good time, and not get emotionally involved. But I suspected that someone very special had broken his heart and that he never healed.

The last weekend that I ever saw Barton, he kept on slipping in and out of consciousness, and was hallucinating. He had around the clock hospice care and the nurses said that having visions was very common when somebody nears the end. Berta was at the point of complete exhaustion and Randy and I both insisted that she go to take a nap, while Fred and my Mom were making further arrangements with the nurses and hospice staff.

In one of those rare moments in which Barton was lucid, he held my hand really tight, and with his eyes tearing and voice cracking, softly said, "Please take care of my dog." I reassured him that we would and I am glad that Barton had seen Sandy and I bond beforehand; to the point that when Sandy once rolled over for me exposing her belly in a playful manner, he said, "She never did that with me, I'm jealous!"

Sandy had been guarding Barton round the clock since his illness and it was very hard for her having all these strangers in her house and all the invasive medical equipment and she wouldn't let anybody near him.

Barton died Monday afternoon. Three months after he was diagnosed with cancer.

When I received the call at work, I left immediately, and could not stop sobbing. Even though we know that somebody is dying, it is still a surprise when they actually do.

When I arrived at Barton's house, there was yellow tape around the front garden, and inside was the coroner, nurses, and other people. His body was not even cold when real estate agents began swarming the desirable property like hungry albatross. Fred and Berta were both dealing with the aftermath, and I went to look for Sandy who was temporarily put in the front bathroom, so that she would not run away with the doors being constantly open, and streams of people entering and exiting the home.

When I opened the bathroom door Sandy looked up and gazed into my eyes and bravely gave me a stoic look that still haunts me to this very day.

The expression in her eyes said it all. She knew and understood everything. She knew Barton was gone.

The bathroom floor was filled with uneaten biscuits, and I tried giving Sandy one more to comfort her, but she just gently took it in her mouth to be polite, and let it drop to the ground.

At that moment, I don't know if I was crying for myself or for Sandy. She completely broke my heart.

I also don't know if dogs believe in such a thing as false hope, but when Sandy was released from the bathroom after all the strangers were gone, she quickly ran out hoping to still find Barton there. It was very, very sad.

Following Barton's death there was a stillness and silence that was almost deafening. I remembered that desolate feeling from the time when my father died suddenly of a massive heart attack. After a long flight to Washington State, where my father had retired, my brother and I drove up to his lush verdant property, arriving at his home without him being there to greet us at the door, and knowing that we would never see him again.

To make this unforeseen situation more bearable, and as an homage to my father, I carefully packed a bunch of white taper candles and put them inside my suitcase before leaving on our trip. At sundown

I handed them out to his wide circle of friends, who where at his memorial, as we stood outside on his woodsy tree lined back yard porch. With the all candles lit up as they each told memorable stories about my father, who was well liked and very funny with an off-beat sense of humor and a deep appreciation for "all things absurd", which I seemed to inherit, I later read one of his long poems, "The Hobo's Retreat." This brought a smile to their faces. I asked everybody to blow out the candles in unison after a countdown, and by that time the sky was a deep midnight blue. The only light around came from the inside of the house.

My father would have liked that so we did something similar for Barton.

The night of Barton's death Sandy did not eat her dinner, and she slept in Berta's room. She vomited a few times afterwards and was grieving and in full mourning. As she lied down, Sandy had her chin on the ground with her paws to the sides of her face and barely looked up.

I took a week off from work so that I could help Fred with the funeral arrangements and memorial, which turned out quite lovely with all of Barton's friends telling stories about him and we got to hear different glimpses to his personality. My mom was a great help in arranging the food and offered her home as a gathering place after the funeral.

But there was little time for mourning now that we had this living, breathing creature to care for, which completely depended on us. Sandy's needs had to be addressed immediately.

We tried to find out if Sandy had all of her vaccines and started sorting through a stack of veterinarian's cards we found inside a drawer, only to find that no one had a record of her. All we really knew about Sandy was the kind of food that she ate at the time.

Berta desperately needed a break and offered to get us her friend Marta for a couple of days while she was still there, so there would be a smooth transition after she left and Sandy would not be alone. Marta ended up staying for several months and only went home on the weekends. This arrangement gave Sandy some time to adjust to life without Barton in a familiar setting. Fred and I went to her Northridge home daily, meeting there after work so that we could continue to bond with Sandy and there would be some consistency in her life and have her feel that she was not going to be abandoned. We would end up eating dinner around ten at night, but it was worth it just seeing her light up when we arrived. On the weekends we went three times a day to keep Sandy company, feed her and let her outside to run in her backyard. We would stay until very late at night when she was already tired and ready for sleep and kept the TV on and soft lighting, as we had done before when Barton was in the hospital. It made me very sad to leave Sandy alone overnight even though Marta would be returning Monday morning just in time to feed her breakfast.

Whenever we entered Sandy's home, her initial greeting was a ritual of circling back and forth around me and herding me in with her nose. As I would sit on the ground then she would lie on her side and swat me with her paws just like a cat, totally adorable. I was especially flattered that Sandy had chosen me to circle around. She only does this with me.

Sandy would later run back to the family room and jump up on one of the twin love seats and sit waiting for one of us to follow her. Usually Fred would go back first and Sandy would get off her love seat and go sit next to him waiting to be petted. After a while she would join me on my love seat. She was the perfect hostess sharing her time with both of us equally.

Marta came up with the great idea of feeding Sandy only half her dinner and having me give her the rest when I got there. It would strengthen our bond.

During her time with Marta, Sandy became bilingual after watching all the Spanish soaps, the telenovelas, from dawn to dusk. They understood each other very well and Marta's calm Zen-like, low-key energy was helpful in comforting and healing Sandy.

As we slowly gained Sandy's trust, her personality started shining through and she began demonstrating more affection and even a dry sense of humor.

Sandy's home was a one story with an open floor plan and a large back yard. Fred and I were beginning to feel guilty about bringing her to our four-story townhouse without a yard, once the packing up was done and the home remodeling was completed, but we couldn't wait to bring Sandy home.

Chapter Two

TRANSITION PERIOD

As we started sorting through Barton's personal belongings, his death made me think of my own mortality. I wondered where I would be, if I would be alone or surrounded by loved ones since we don't have children, would I be ill or just die of old age? I had so many questions.

We put aside all the family photos in boxes, and Fred became very sentimental, nostalgic and melancholic, feeling overwhelmed with grief. It hadn't been too long since he had buried his own mother after a very lengthy illness and later his father, who died shortly after Bernice.

We kept all of Barton's vinyl records and music collection of which he was very proud, and other things that had belonged to Aunt Sally, and now have them scattered throughout our home to keep them both close by. Other things ended up in public storage until we had time to decide what to do with them. Little by little we gave away pieces of his life to Berta and Marta, and various charities until the house was completely empty. It is a monumental task to clear a home worth of a lifetime of possessions from somebody else's life.

I asked myself "Is this it, do our lives end up in public storage, or in thrift shops?" "Will our belongings have any meaning to complete strangers?" "Will they appreciate the same things that we held dear to our hearts?" And ultimately, "What kind of person will end up with our possessions?"

I prefer to believe that there is a positive side to all of this, and that in a way we live on through what once was ours, and now belongs to somebody else.

Fred and I were not blessed with children, but in time we came to appreciate the upside of being childless. We were free to come and go as we pleased and we didn't have to put anybody through college. And then along came Sandy.

As hard as it's been to raise her, Sandy has also been the biggest blessing in our lives. She has completed us as individuals and has given us a sense of purpose that was missing before. In a way she has forced both Fred and I to finally grow up and to have the same responsibilities and obligations that human parents have.

Now our lives completely revolve around Sandy because she is our number one priority, and that is the way we want it. As a result I have given up one of my favorite hobbies in the entire universe, and that is to travel.

I figured that the rest of the world would still be waiting for me to discover someday in the far future, but for now my place was to be home with Sandy.

I knew that after everything she had been through, that I could not leave her even for a week, even if she was home with Fred, or with my mom, and risk her feeling that she had been abandoned yet one more time.

First she lost Sally, then Barton and now her home, the only one she had ever known. It was going to take Sandy a very long period to adjust to her new life and build trust between us all, and any kind of change would upset her new routine. She needed stability and a sense of security and continuity.

I am grateful that I had the opportunity to travel a great deal while in my early twenties. During my college years I worked every weekend so that I could earn enough money to pay for my own trips and I considered this to be the greatest gift from me to me. It gave me a feeling of self-accomplishment and more confidence. Traveling opened a whole other door for me, and I learned that getting there was half the adventure and that one has to travel with an open mind and heart.

There is nothing like walking the pavement, hearing the sounds, smelling the air and tasting the food while in a different country, as well as the anticipation and excitement of the unexpected.

My first trip to Europe included England, France, Italy, Holland, Germany and Austria. With my high school best friend Kathy, I went on a student tour, which I thought was my best option at the time since I only had a month off from work and I wanted to see and learn as much as possible in that time frame, instead of buying a Eurail Pass and doing it on our own. We had a fabulous time and met some wonderful people along the way.

A couple of years later Kathy and I would take a road trip across country from California to Massachusetts where she moved to be close to her grandparents and cousins and I flew back home. It was mid October and the perfect time of year for this trip as we saw the fall season change from state to state. When we reached Pennsylvania the roads were completely covered with a carpet of millions of fall leaves ranging from deep amber to russet and burgundy red. I was in so much awe of this unbelievably beautiful scene that I made Kathy stop the car in the middle of the road since there was nobody behind us, or in front for that matter, and I filled a bag with leaves to take back home as a souvenir. I later carefully pinned these leaves to my bedroom wall in the shape of a tree.

The second overseas trip that I took was with my cousin Sorel who was going to college in Montreal at the time. Her mother, my Aunt Blanca, had recently and suddenly passed away from a brain hemorrhage and I felt it would be a good time for Sorel to get away and give herself a time to heal, so I invited her to join me on this journey. We met in New York where our connecting flight was supposed to take us to Spain, and eventually to Portugal and Morocco. But there was a sudden airline strike and

I had to switch airplanes once I arrived at LAX and found myself running across the airport with my suitcase to catch another flight. That is when the real adventure started.

When I got to New York, Sorel was already waiting for me at Kennedy Airport but we missed our connecting flight to Europe by only a few minutes, because my flight in LA had been delayed in taking off. I had no luggage because it had been sent directly to Spain. Sorel and I spent the night in New York and we stayed with our Aunt Renee who lived there and she loaned me some pajamas. I had to wear the same clothes the next day, which was a new and uncomfortable experience for me, but decided to go with the flow being the situation was unpredictable.

The next morning after a fantastic home cooked breakfast, our aunt drove us to the airport and we got into a minor car accident. We almost missed our flight to Spain again, where our tour was waiting for us. I was really happy to finally see my luggage but ironically Sorel's was missing, and kept on following us from country to country for the duration of the trip. I felt really bad for her because she had just bought clothes in New York and did not get them until after the trip was over. She was a really good sport about it however, determined not to let it spoil her trip. When we finally caught up with the rest of our tour, everybody offered to loan her clothes, but for a few days she wore the same v-neck knit dress which she washed nightly until it stretched out so much she could no longer wear it. I loaned Sorel some shoes when I found out we wore the same size and eventually she bought some mix and match pieces that would work well in the arid weather.

On the way to the hotel, we had a crazy Spaniard taxi driver, who was trying to take us to a nudist beach, which are apparently very popular in Europe, but we politely declined his invitation. Since our fellow travelers were out sightseeing we decided to spend the majority of the day visiting the Prado Museum in Madrid. We visited Sevilla and Granada and Salamanca among other places, and at the end of our tour Sorel and I went off by ourselves to the Costa del Sol specifically to see Torremolinos, which I had read about in the James A. Michener novel "The Drifters."

One of my funniest memories of Spain is when Sorel and I were at a train station in Malaga by ourselves and the captain was making lewd remarks about us, saying "those American girls", to another male even though we are modest in our way of dressing. Unbeknownst to him that both of us were completely bilingual and understood everything that he said. Sorel was totally mortified, but my nature being a little on the feisty side, could not resist going up to him, looking him strait in the eye and ask him in Spanish how long of a wait for the next train. The look on his face was priceless.

I cannot express the excitement that I felt when we were crossing the Straight of Gibraltar on a ferryboat to enter into the North African continent on our way to Morocco. And once we had reached our destination I could not get over the elegance in Morocco and how we were served our meals with waiters beautifully dressed in costume with the Fez hats and white gloves.

I was also pleasantly surprised by the warmth, hospitality and charm of its people because on my previous trip to Europe, much to my disappointment, I found several countries to have been very anti-American with people often making comments such as "you Americans think you can buy anything with your dirty money." In one instance we had gone to what appeared to be a very nice restaurant for lunch and after waiting for more than fifteen minutes without anybody approaching us with a menu, our lovely Swiss tour guide Sabine, went to see what was going on. There were only a few patrons seated who were already eating, so it was not as if they were very busy and they certainly had enough waiters, so we ended up leaving when Sabine confirmed our suspicions.

While in Morocco, we got to ride on camels in the vast endless desert, walk through a Kasbah and Medina, and visit magical opulent palaces straight out of "Arabian Nights." The heady scent of jasmine and sweet mint tea and exotic spices combined with the oppressive heat was intoxicating. Adding to the intensity of this experience was an eerie buzz one could hear around five times a day, enveloping the city, much like a swarm of bees, but it was its people praying towards Mecca. Very haunting.

During a visit to the ancient flea market while Sorel and I were trying on various caftans, I was writing some notes and the merchant became fascinated with my ballpoint pen. He offered to trade it for a beautifully handcrafted vase and I quickly accepted his offer. We were both happy with our new treasures, but I could not understand why he found value in something so commercial and manufactured. I have always loved and appreciated folk art because a lot of heart and soul goes into turning an ordinary object into an extraordinary one, with its vivid imagination and colorful, detailed-oriented designs.

When I returned home, a seasoned traveler, and shared some of my stories with my father he said, "you'll never get lost" and I knew then that he was right. That no matter where in the world I would be, that I would feel right at home.

Over the years, while still single, I would also travel to Puerto Vallarta and Acapulco, to Vancouver and Victoria in British Columbia and to Tegucigalpa and the Mayan ruins of Copan in Honduras. Once married, the very last trips that Fred and I went on before we inherited Sandy would be to Michigan, as guests of a radio station that carried Fred's show. Later, one of our most memorable trips was for our five-year wedding anniversary to Colonial Williamsburg in Virginia where we spent a very magical Thanksgiving. After that we went to

Guatemala twice, where I spent my early childhood from the ages of two to twelve. I am glad Fred got to experience that and he loved the country, its people and the food, but got the impression that all people do there was to eat and party, because we went there over the holidays and another time for a very lavish wedding.

Sure I was going to miss the excitement of discovering new countries and the opportunity for personal growth, but for now it will suffice that I have a lifetime full of wonderful memories, which are as crystal clear as if it were just yesterday. Now I was about to embark on a different sort of journey and adventure raising Sandy, and I wouldn't miss out on it or trade it for anything in the world. I wanted her to also feel right at home.

Chapter Three

WEEKEND FROM HELL

What happened during that long three-day weekend can only be summed as, in by Friday, out by Monday.

Fred and I were really excited about Sandy's move into our home and into our lives for good, and I had taken that Friday off from work to help her have a smooth transition through yet another period of adjustment.

We had arranged for the new dog trainer to meet us at Sandy's house to help drive her to our place, because Sandy would not let us put a collar and leash around her neck and we could not get her into the car. She carried Sandy who rode inside her car and we followed them behind with all of Sandy's belongings, which had been carefully packed the night before by Marta, who would be returning back to her home.

As soon as we arrived at our townhouse we realized that Sandy would be faced with many challenges that we did not anticipate such as climbing a flight of stairs, which she had never done before. The simple things that we take for granted would prove to be very trying experiences for her. Just getting her down to the foyer and back up to the living room became close to impossible without outside help. Getting Sandy outside to the common area for her bathroom needs was even harder and also not working out, and I then realized that we expect so much from animals to understand what we need from them, when we ourselves had to be taught everything as toddlers. Just as we learned in baby steps what to do, they as well had to be taught how to be potty trained on various surfaces such as grass, dirt, and cement.

What we had envisioned as a blissful ever after, was quickly turning into a nightmare, when we realized that we could not manage her. Once it dawned on Sandy that this was not a visit and this place was not her usual home, the honeymoon was over, and she quickly went from playful to depressed and lost her appetite, refusing to eat and even drink water. She was agitated, fearful and worst of all unhappy.

Sandy had also not relieved herself for forty-eight hours straight, despite our many efforts to get her to go outside, and we were extremely worried. I had made several attempts to carry her downstairs to no avail. She was very stressed out and would get aggressive and snap at me. Finally when Sandy could no longer hold it, while sitting on our couch, she suddenly jumped down and peed on our brand new carpet, making a huge puddle.

Fred became so upset and frustrated that he went upstairs into our bedroom, closed the door and did not come out for the rest of the afternoon. Very dramatic, in true Fred fashion. I did not mind cleaning up her mess, because it was hers, and the maternal side of me forgives many things, and tried my best not to make Sandy feel bad.

We did not know what to do. How were we going to make this all work out? For an unthinkable minute we even contemplated giving her away to a Sheltie rescue, with people who were experienced with her breed, because we felt this living situation was unfair to her.

All I know is that if Sandy, God forbid, had somehow ended up in an animal shelter, she would have not passed any of the tests and would be deemed unadoptable and I hate to even imagine what her fate might have been.

But in reality thinking about all those crazy things was not even an option. After all Sandy was now family and we were going to make it work out no matter what. We also promised a dying man we would take care of his dog and there was no turning back. Once I make a promise I seldom change my mind unless the circumstances prevent me from keeping it. Fred's values are pretty much the same despite our enormous differences.

We both desperately wanted the new situation to work out and I called my mom in tears for her advice. She suggested that we take Sandy back to her Northridge home temporarily, and to get Marta back in order to buy us more time, until we were all ready to live together again. After all Barton's house still needed some remodeling before it could be put on the market to be sold. Fred agreed that it was a good idea although he too became misty eyed and guilty at the thought of sending Sandy back to her home. As I started to pack her belongings, Fred pulled out and kept her yellow ball and placed it on the couch where he watched TV, until her return.

Monday morning while I was back at work, my mom made arrangements to meet Marta at Sandy's home before we would arrive that evening. I had already packed most of Sandy's things the night before so the move could go as smoothly as possible. Getting Sandy into our car was another story, and I had to carefully choreograph pulling the car up to the front door, leaving the door open, and luring her down to the foyer with a leash, out the door and having her jump inside without any interruptions. It had to be done in one take, as they say. Otherwise she would have frozen with fear and would try to back out.

When Sandy arrived at her familiar home she was ecstatic. She ran throughout the entire house rubbing her body against the furniture and rugs reclaiming her territory and climbed up on the couch in the den where she used to watch TV with Marta and literally kicked up her heels belly up.

The change in her disposition was like night and day and we knew we had made the right decision for the moment.

We decided to start the home remodeling on the outside first, so it would make the situation livable during the time that Sandy and Marta would became roommates again, and it would also give us a few months to get her some in home training.

Sometimes it takes a perfect stranger to point out what we fail to see in ourselves. Until I was repeatedly told how patient I was with Sandy, I had never given it much thought before. Nobody has the kind of patience that I apparently have. It may well be my only virtue.

I had taken on the role of mentor to Sandy, sort of like Professor Higgins to her Eliza Doolittle, from the play "Pygmalion" or the better known movie "My Fair Lady" with my all time favorite movie star Audrey Hepburn. I was determined to turn Sandy's life around through thick and thin.

One of my colleagues at the time overheard a phone conversation I was having with a friend during my lunchtime, and he later asked me why I tried so hard with Sandy who was obviously a problem dog. He said if it were he, he already would have dropped her off to the nearest animal shelter, and said, "she is just a dog." I replied that I could not do that because first of all she was a family member, that I loved her, and that I promised Barton before he died that we would adopt her and take care of her and that I keep my promises. Aside from that Sandy would be deemed unadoptable by shelter standards because she was fearful, aggressive as a result, distrustful and touch sensitive among other things and would have failed the temperament testing done beforehand. Nobody would have invested the time and patience to deal with her issues and later find out that she is in reality the sweetest dog in the entire world. A dog like that no matter how beautiful, gets put down first. He then had the gall to tell me that "Barton wouldn't know, after all he is dead" and I replied, "but I know."

I found his insensitive and crass comments particularly offensive and disrespectful, and since I really had not asked him for his unsolicited advice, I gave him a piece of my mind. By saying, "instead of worrying about what I do with my dog who has been through so much grief outliving two of her human parents and losing her home and my efforts to give her a happy and healthy life, maybe you should take your drunk driving teenage daughter who got arrested, to the teenage pound. Maybe there she could learn the values that you never taught her, so she wouldn't need to find solace in a bottle of alcohol. After all she is a repeat offender who has been extremely lucky not to have been caught."

Needless to say he was stunned and speechless at my spitfire retort and to my surprise later softly said, "You're right." I wondered why a pretty seventeen year old girl who was a good student and popular was so unhappy and what would the future hold for her is she was this wayward now.

What was so perplexing was that she had a loving mother, who raised her and her siblings whom she was very close with. I never suspected that there was any kind of abuse between her and her father since there seemed to be a genuine affection between them, without any hesitation or hostility. Half of the population has divorced parents and not all their children display such antics. My question was why are some children in the same family okay while others are not? Are they born with a self-destructive gene or is it just growing pains, trying to get negative attention, or was it peer pressure or maybe she was just a self indulgent spoiled brat who was used to having her messes constantly cleaned up and swept under the carpet?

What was most disturbing of all was that she had previously injured an undocumented immigrant while driving under the influence. She paid him off in cash for his minor injuries and her only comment was "he did not have the right to be on the road because he is illegal." With a feeling of entitlement and superiority, she was in complete denial of any wrongdoing. What if she had killed him? Would she have considered his life to be less valuable because he was undocumented?

I followed with "I'll make a deal with you, I'll take care of my troubled dog and you take care of your troubled daughter who is crying out for help to deaf ears. For her sake I hope that you and your family can get to the root of her problem before it's too late." But what I really meant is "you stay out of my backyard and I'll stay out of yours." For so many years of my life I was the consummate diplomat, always being careful about what I said and to whom, until I came to the conclusion that being diplomatic was a complete waste of time. Telling it like it is, is more in keeping with my true nature. I may be a lot of things good or bad, but I am not a phony.

Chapter Four

HOMECOMING AT LAST

In anticipation of Sandy's permanent arrival, I was fine-tuning my efforts to dog proof our home, and to make a more dog-friendly environment for her. Since we did not have a yard in our townhome, I decided to create a makeshift garden for Sandy with a patch of grass that I bought from the garden center nearby. I packed the flats of sod inside an empty sandbox from the toy store and placed it outside in our living room balcony, which was a flight up from the foyer.

The clerk at the store had said, "let me help you to the car because the sod is a little bit heavy." Did he say "a little bit heavy?" When I tried to get it out of the trunk, it felt like a ton of bricks. I could not move it. So I went inside the house, got a large garbage bag and I carefully slipped the sod inside the bag, but still could not get it out of the car and only after a long struggle I finally managed to push it out, slide it across the pavement and drag it up the flight of stairs. That thing weighed more than I did. I had opened the balcony door beforehand so that I could just do it all in one trip. Fred tried to help, while standing at the top of the stairs, but I frantically screamed, "Everybody, out of the way, out of the way, I am going to lose my momentum and fall back." Sandy was very excited and curious about all the commotion, started barking and went outside to the balcony to investigate her new yard, which I was very proud of.

Every night I would water her new garden, but it wasn't long before my brilliant idea turned into a swampy mess replete with mosquitoes. This of course was during the beginning of the West Nile Virus, thus triggering Fred's paranoia.

One day after work, I walked into a very strange chemical smell permeating throughout the house. I said, "Fred, did somebody fumigate around here?"

"No, I sprayed mosquito repellant" he said proudly.

"Why?"

"Three words, Sand"

"Three words?"

"Three words!"

Suddenly I felt I was in the middle of a quiz show, and if I answered correctly I would win a prize. Either that or Fred was doing a cheap imitation of Regis Philbin.

"West Nile Virus!"

"West Nile Virus?"

"We are all going to die"

"We are?" I said humoring him as I often do.

"Haven't you heard Sand?"

"We have West Nile Virus in the San Fernando Valley?"

Fred just rolled his eyes and walked away shaking his head.

I was convinced that Fred was certifiable, although in the course of our long marriage I am sure that Fred has thought the same of me, at least on one occasion, or two. I waited for the hysteria to subside.

A newspaper sportswriter in LA, used to refer to Fred as "the king of paranoia", in many of his articles. A quality Fred often exhibited during his radio broadcasts. What the columnist doesn't know is that that is the biggest understatement of all time and does not do justice to Fred. Not only is my Freddie the "king of paranoia", but he has also elevated it to an art form. You have to live with it to believe it. To anybody who is familiar with the old TV show "The Odd Couple", Fred is a combination of Oscar Madison and Felix Unger all rolled up into one. A handful!

I thought our chances of dying were far greater after breathing in the toxic fumes from the insect repellant spray inside our home, rather than from the West Nile Virus itself, especially in southern California at the time. Ironically, with all of the home foreclosures four years later, the swimming pools of abandoned homes tested positive for the virus. Fred was ahead of his time, God bless him.

However, I was glad that Sandy was already on preventative heartworm medication. The vet told us early on that when infected mosquitoes bite animals, they deposit eggs into the bloodstream, which then later turn into heartworms, which is a devastating disease. Many dogs were afflicted with heartworm during the Katrina catastrophe and it is a lengthy and difficult treatment, but heartworm has been known to also cause death.

In order to diffuse the panic, I brought some dirt back from Barton's backyard while it was being landscaped and remodeled so that it would have a familiar scent for Sandy. When I got home I packed it onto the sandbox over the rotten sod until all the moisture was gone and the sun did the rest of the job. Voila, no more mosquitoes!

Shortly after Sandy moved in, Fred received a phone call that I answered and it went something like this.

"Hello?"

"Sorry, I have the wrong number"

"Why do you say that?"

"Because there is a dog barking"

"You have the right number"

"Is this Fred Wallin's house?"

"Yes"

"Fred has a dog?"

"That's right"

"Fred Wallin has a dog!"

"Yes he does"

"I don't believe it"

"Believe it!"

"Fred, the radio guy?"

"The very same Fred"

"I'll be darned!"

"Fred is on his way to becoming an enlightened man, he may even reach nirvana one day if he plays his cards right!"

"I'll be darned!"

"What is the dog's name?"

"Sandy"

"And what is your name?"

"Sandy"

I did not want to go through another interrogation so I spared him and said,

"We inherited her, and we both had the same name, and there is no point in changing her name because we want to avoid an identity crisis. Do you still want to speak with Fred?"

"No, I forgot why I called. I'll call back later"

"Sand, did I hear the phone ring?"

"Wrong number!"

I just did not have the energy to explain, and I knew he would be calling back.

In an effort to socialize Sandy we always left her balcony door open so that she could hear and bark at the other dogs in the townhouse complex, and see them from far away on her walks in the common area. But she was just terrified of going outside. It was almost impossible to get her out the front door. We had previously made several attempts to take Sandy to the park where Fred and I used to walk before we inherited her, because we thought that she might enjoy it. After all most dogs love it. We first went on a quiet Sunday afternoon, because weekdays were very hectic there, with too many dogs and people running around. But it proved to be sheer torture for her as she was completely petrified. Sandy's anxiety level was so high that she peed about ten times, and her nose was dripping from pure fear. She couldn't wait to get back home and started pulling me towards the car. We realized that the world was too big for her, especially after being sheltered for so long, and decided not to put her through that agony again.

We thought that it might be good for Sandy if we had more people over and started to entertain more often in smaller groups at a time. At first she would bark at the company then she would go and hide in her new safe spot behind the coffee table. As time went on and Sandy developed more self-confidence, she herded our guests into a corner. I was so proud of her that in their presence I said "good little sheepdog!" Our guests did not share our enthusiasm and were not exactly amused. We haven't heard from them in a long, long time. Oh, well.

People have often suggested that we get a companion dog for Sandy, but she is not accustomed to being around other pets and is used to being the only one, and I am not about to make Sandy feel second best in her own home. Aside from that, she is a handful, equivalent to ten human children. I did not know who was more high maintenance, Fred or Sandy

"The Sheltie." Besides, there is always someone home with her, be it Fred who works out of the house, and me when I come home and on the weekends. If we are both gone it is not for more than two to four hours at a time. We both try to spend as much time as possible with Sandy and have often passed up invitations to parties, dinners, weddings, travel and other gatherings that would take us away from her for a long time. We'd rather be home with Sandy.

Friends also suggested that we change her name but I was not about to strip Sandy of her identity at this stage in her life. They thought it would help to avoid confusion regarding the two Sandy's, but I reassured them there is none whatsoever. When Fred speaks to Sandy "The Sheltie", it is always a little softer and a lot sweeter.

Fred who had never had a dog in his life and had zero experience with animals, soon became the doting proud father, oftentimes calling me at work to tell me how smart, intuitive, beautiful and astounding Sandy is.

Of course I already knew all that. Fred also discovered how funny she is, especially when people sneeze, she can't stand it and gets up and moves away while glaring at us as if we had done something wrong. He was also totally impressed by her sense of time. She knows when it is a weekend and when it is a holiday!

Fred had also found his TV buddy, enjoying Sandy's company sitting side by side on the couch watching all the games to prepare for his radio show, which is a huge part of Fred's job. Working out of the house can be very lonely and he really appreciated her presence and sometimes even her input, as Sandy would often bark at some of the teams on the screen. She made Fred laugh and brought a great deal of happiness to his life as well as mine.

That is when I found out that Fred was also sharing the triple ginger cookies with Sandy that he would buy on his weekly hunting expeditions to Trader Joes, where he would return home with a vast array of cookies, cookies and more cookies. Less is more was never a part of Fred's dictionary. One would think that we lived in a remote village in the Andes where there are no markets nearby, by the volume of "supplies" Fred would buy! Even though Sandy loved those cookies, wagging her tail with great anticipation, they are way too rich for dogs and I suggested Fred stick to her biscuits and in moderation and also not to eat in front of her because he was not able to resist those eyes, always giving in to her.

Sandy had Fred completely wrapped around her little paws. Realizing this habit was hard to break I found myself confiscating the cookies on several occasions. Not only did I have to train Sandy, I had to train Fred as well.

As we got to know Sandy better, we discovered she is the smartest, most inquisitive and alert dog we have ever met. No person, piece of mail, parcel, newspaper, grocery bag, or clothing etc. is allowed into the house without a thorough nose scanning and inspection from her. Sandy is a combination of Inspectress Clousou, Colombo and Sherlock Holmes, but mostly she is a busy body. She has to know everything! But as far as her nose scanning skills are concerned, Sandy is hands down the best there is in the business.

One day I noticed that our couch began to look different but I couldn't quite figure out why, until I got up close and saw a lot of holes with white fiberfill exposed. I told Fred that we might have a moth problem, although we never had one before, and was about to schedule an appointment with an exterminator, when the evidence was hanging out the sides of the culprit's mouth. Sandy had the gull to pretend she had done absolutely nothing wrong, with an angelic look across her face, which is hard to resist.

When I approached Sandy and tried to pull the fiberfill out of her mouth, she started showing some major teeth and began hissing like a snake, becoming extremely protective and territorial of the couch, barking and lunging at us and would not let us near it. I was worried that she would have intestinal blockage because she had been secretly chewing it for some time, so I called the vet and he told me what signs to look out for, but that probably she would pass it. We could not understand the cause of Sandy's aggressive behavior and only after reading several books discovered she was in "mine" mode. And I thought that she was going through "the terrible two's" again!

I tried several chew deterrents to spray on the couch but none of them worked. Underneath it all, I really didn't mind that she was chewing on Fred's couch from his bachelor days, which we had been meaning to replace for some time. My only concern was her safety. It took a lot of experimenting with the right chews and toys to slowly eliminate that problem over a period of time.

Fred and I read as many books on dog behavior, health and care as we possibly could, watched TV shows on training as well as videos, and realized that Sandy pretty much was the poster child for every behavioral problem in the book. She was our problem child, with many issues, but in our hearts could do no wrong no matter what, and after several months it became very evident that Sandy had Fred and I very well trained. Anybody who truly believes that their pets don't run their lives is in complete denial.

One major problem that we could not get rid of was Sandy's excessive barking. At one point Sandy decided she was going to co-host Fred's radio show and barked right in the middle of it. There are only so many excuses that Fred can give on her behalf while trying to make a joke about it to his audience.

That same week Fred had been particularly upset because a long time caller on his show finally agreed with him after ten years of heated debated banter. He felt that "it is over between us, the dynamic is gone." Just like in that famous Victor Hugo novel "Les Miserables", where the fugitive prisoner Valjean finally gets caught but Inspector Javert lets him go, after the years-long pursuit felt like a letdown. Realizing that Fred can only be happy when he is miserable, I reassured him that the combative caller would eventually disagree with him again. Fred wasn't convinced but there is only so much indulging that I can do before I reach my cut off point, and that is called self-preservation.

Another time while I was at work I received a frantic call from Fred saying he could not leave the house because Sandy had vomited at the base of the stairs and would not let him through to the foyer. I had noticed in the past that on the few occasions she had previously done that, she had become very guarded, aggressive and possessive of her vomit and the vet had explained that as disgusting as it seems to us, animals consider their vomit to be a source of food, and want it back. It is a primal instinct. I relayed this to Fred and told him that she was in another form of "mine mode", and suggested to him that he throw a treat at the far opposite direction of where she was, so that he would have time to run down and block her with the baby gate, but he was just not fast enough for her.

When Sandy has gotten aggressive she is reminiscent of a small wolf, with the speed of the roadrunner. Fred made several attempts to no avail, and to make a long story shorter, our beloved little Sheltie who is no higher than a foot and a half, held six foot Fred hostage in his own home.

When I got home, Sandy was still guarding her vomit, so I pretended that I didn't notice it and passed right by her without making eye contact. When she was finally in a more relaxed state, and didn't see me as a threat, I threw a treat outside into her balcony and waited for her to fetch and eat it and quickly closed the screen door until I was able to clean up her mess. Once it was gone she forgot all about it and was back to her sweet old self just like a child who has been given a pacifier after a long tantrum.

One evening while Fred was downstairs watching TV in our living room he asked me if I had just given Sandy something to chew on. I was in the kitchen on the second level and as I stood at the edge of the steps looking down I could see Sandy guarding her "prey." As I came closer she started to snarl at me and get aggressive and I noticed that she had stolen a ballpoint pen from the coffee table and proceeded to chew on it. I tried in vain to get her to drop it, and the more I tried to distract her the faster she chewed on it. Fred and I were screaming at her to stop and tried to get her other treats but she was rapidly chewing and swallowing the entire pen. We were both hysterical and I was crying thinking she was going to get poisoned and die from the ink. I ran back up to the kitchen to get the Yellow Pages and was frantically searching for an emergency vet nearby. Fred suggested that we don't waste any time but just to get going and to take the phone book with. He helped me to lure Sandy downstairs to the foyer with a piece of turkey, and stayed with her, while I got the car out of the garage and parked it at the front door so I could just run in, give her another piece of turkey so I could put a leash on her and get her inside the car. She was delirious and panting heavily as I sat next to her in the back seat while Fred drove. I found and called a 24-hour animal hospital to alert them that we were on our way and luckily it was less than a ten-minute drive.

When we arrived they took x-rays to determine how big the pieces of pen were and whether to induce vomiting or perform surgery, because she could puncture her insides if the edges were too sharp or blunt or too large or she could choke. Since Sandy still had a full stomach from her dinner, which served as a cushion, and she had chewed up the pen in little pieces surprisingly without the ink leaking out, the vet was able to induce vomiting with an amorphine injection until her stomach was empty.

When Sandy was released from the emergency room she looked just like a juvenile delinquent you see on TV, with her head down, not making eye contact, and the only thing that was missing was the orange jumpsuit that you see them wear.

At least she had the decency of looking genuinely ashamed. I stayed home from work the next day to keep an eye on her.

Chapter Five

UPSTAIRS, DOWNSTAIRS

It all started around 3:00 AM when a sound broke through my dreams. Yelp . . . Yelp . . . Yelp, Yelp . . . Triple yelp? . . . . Bark, Bark, Baaarrrk!!!!

"Sand?"

"Who, me?"

"Sand, don't you think you should go downstairs and see what is going on?"

"Not really, I am trying to get some sleep"

"So am I, and so is the entire neighborhood"

"The neighbors are all complaining about Sandy's constant barking during the day, I don't want any problems"

"Fred it is three in the morning, besides I am not the one who is barking. I have a better idea. Why don't you go down?"

"Because you are her mother, and only you can calm her down"

"Please Sand, please"

I couldn't argue with that, so I grabbed my pillows and blankets and huffed and puffed my way down three flights of stairs and set up camp in the middle of our living room floor.

I actually found sleeping on the plush carpet more comfortable than on our squeaky couch from Fred's bachelor days, which we had been threatening to change for years, but didn't get around to doing so, until much later.

Sandy was thrilled to see me and circled and circled around me, wagging her tail, and quickly fell into a deep slumber while she slept on the couch. I was so envious of that.

Once I was down there, I thought this is not that bad, and I could really use a break from Fred's snoring, but soon after I said to myself, how is it possible that I can still hear him snoring all the way down here?

It wasn't Fred!

I had tried unsuccessfully to wean Sandy from my sleeping downstairs with her, and was exhausted from having constant interrupted sleep, which gave me a feeling of "jet-lag", that I finally decided it would just be easier for everybody if I slept downstairs from now on.

Our neighbors were certainly happier, and Sandy felt safe and was becoming more self-confident and better behaved. It made sense since dogs are pack animals and I was part of her pack and they all sleep together.

Sandy has the cutest and quirky habit of "making her nest" before bedtime. She is very finicky and fastidious about exactly how it should be and spends a great deal of time and energy smoothing out her blankets, just so, bunching them up and actually counting strokes, taking turns on each side, with her paws. Then after all that decides to sleep elsewhere! This behavior stems from thousands of years back when her ancestors used to sleep in the open outdoors, never knowing when predators would approach their pack, and making their nest as big as possible with leaves and branches, oftentimes protected them.

It would have been nice to be able to snuggle with Sandy especially on cold winter nights, but being a sheepdog she wanted no part in that. Sandy gets hot quickly with all that long double coat fur and needs to be free. She has refused all these years to be my lap dog.

Fred would occasionally join us downstairs, but did not have the fortitude required to commit to this sacrifice long term and sleeping on the couch was not good for his back. It became our ritual where I would say goodnight to Fred upstairs and I would then tuck our Sheltie downstairs. We were becoming what is considered a dysfunctional family, the three of us, but we were okay with it. After all it worked for us.

It finally occurred to me that is was time to buy a twin bed, which fit perfectly well in a cozy corner nook of our spacious living room, near the fireplace and bookcases, and dressed it up with a nice blanket and colorful pillows and it made for a great reading place as well. It became my favorite spot to read the voluminous Sunday newspaper while Fred and Sandy watched the games on TV sitting side by side on the couch. It was family time.

People would ask us why don't we just bring Sandy upstairs to sleep in our bedroom. My answer would always be "how many hours do you have?"

The main issue was that from the beginning, Sandy had trouble climbing the stairs, and although we tried to lure her all the way up with all kinds of goodies, she was petrified and would not take the bait. Sandy would not let herself be carried, and would literally turn into a wolf when I tried. It has taken me many years to learn how to do so without Sandy attempting to bite me. I also was not going to take a chance and drop her down all those flights of steps, because I knew that she would try to wriggle out of my arms and put up a good fight if I even tried!

Chapter Six

TRAINERS

Soon after Barton's death, while Sandy was going through the transition period in her Northridge house with Marta, I came across a business card for a dog behaviorist at a pet supply shop. I knew Sandy desperately needed training because she was completely unmanageable, and would often act out in aggression, which later on we came to understand as fear motivated.

Over a period of time there was a succession of dog trainers going through a revolving door, reminiscent of the nannies in "Mary Poppins" and "Mrs. Doubtfire." I will refer to all trainers by number only, since I did not really care for any of them.

When we first met trainer #1, she brought along her dog Blitz, another Sheltie, that she uses in her training sessions to help socialize other dogs. Given Sandy's shy nature, we weren't sure how she was going to react, and when Blitz first walked into her house Sandy didn't quite know what to make out of her. I don't know if Sandy had ever even seen another dog in her life, and she quickly ran into her bedroom's safe spot next to her bed hoping that Blitz would go away.

As the trainer and Blitz approached Sandy, she started trembling, and her ears soon fell backward which we learned was a sign of pure fear. Trainer #1 gave us some tips on reading dogs body language so we would learn when and how to approach Sandy.

In the meantime, Blitz, a very lively, curious, and energetic dog went into Sandy's room and pulled out all of her toys, one at a time, hoping to play, but Sandy wasn't interested, and was not possessive about her toys as most animals are.

Trainer #1 suggested that we take Sandy to her vet for a general check up and give her only booster shots just in case she was already vaccinated. We had been trying to do that for the past couple of weeks but could not get Sandy on a collar and leash and we could not get her into a car. The trainer offered to help us get Sandy there, and picked up a tranquilizer from the vet the night before hoping that it would relax her and make that trip less traumatic, especially with all the sudden changes in her life. Now I know that a good trainer would have never tried giving Sandy a pill and instead would have used gentle coaxing as a way to calm her down.

The next morning the trainer attempted to give Sandy the pill inside a piece of cheese, but I told her that she was not used to eating cheese and might get sick. She said it was worth a try, but when Sandy did not take the bait, the trainer became impatient, and along with Blitz cornered Sandy in her "safe room" and turned her over on her back trying to shove the pill down her throat. At the time I knew absolutely nothing about dog training but I knew this was terribly wrong and immediately raised a red flag in my mind. I was very upset and started to distrust the trainer and questioned her methods. I did not care that she got offended and I asked her to stop immediately. The trainer tried to reassure me that she knew what she was doing, but she had already lost me. I was really happy when Sandy asserted herself and bit the trainer in her hand causing her to bleed and to feel embarrassed at her lack of professionalism. Although the trainer made light of the dog bite saying that it is part of her job, Sandy taught her a lesson and it was very humbling. I was even happier when Blitz mistakenly ate the piece of cheese that contained the tranquilizer. As a last resort the trainer decided to put a towel over Sandy and managed to carry and put her inside the car's front seat while Blitz started to fall asleep, fully stretched out on the back seat. She was really out of it.

I followed them to the vet in my car but when we arrived the doctor was feeling very ill with the flu and was only capable of doing a very short examination. The vet tech gave Sandy her vaccines and said she was sure that Sandy had been spayed because she felt a small scar in her pelvic area. As far as we were concerned we were set.

Fred and I decided to give trainer #1 the benefit of the doubt and another chance at working with

Sandy, because she had come through in other areas. She started with trying to put a prong collar on as a way of training Sandy to walk properly without pulling. I would soon find out that this method is considered controversial and should only be used for very short periods of time and only by people who are very well experienced to use it. Since Fred and I were not capable of hooking the collar on or off without Sandy snapping and lunging at us, the trainer suggested that we keep it on her at all times, including while she slept, until our next session.

When we tried to pet Sandy she became very irritable and hostile. We realized that she was sensitive in the neck area and was in pain from the collar that was pinching her even through her very thick fur. We immediately called the trainer, but could not reach her on Sunday night despite the many calls so we called the vet the next morning. The vet was very alarmed about the suggestion her friend, the trainer, had made and said for us to remove the collar immediately and to never use it again. But we could not do it. Every time I made an attempt Sandy nipped at me. Both of us tried for several hours to reach the trainer again until we finally got a hold of her and relayed what the vet had told us. She disagreed with the vet and both of us and insisted again that she knew what she was doing and that the collar would not hurt Sandy, but I was not willing to give her another chance ever again. I told her that I wanted the collar off and that she needed to come over right away.

As patient as I am, once I make up my mind about somebody or something it is over for good. I don't mind burning bridges.

I went back to the pet store where I first found the business card and told the shop owner what had happened and he removed her cards from his counter and threw them away. He was very surprised and shocked and above all very disappointed.

A few weeks later we started working with trainer #2 who was referred to us by a friend who has worked with him. He was more experienced, had written a book, and is quite well known among the circle of trainers. After our first bad experience, I needed to make sure that the trainer be legitimate and not a fraud with a cute business card claiming to be a behaviorist. Apparently there are only a few legitimate ones with a PhD in the country. We decided to book three, very expensive, one-hour sessions over three Saturday's at Sandy's Northridge home and we had exercises to practice during the week.

He taught us how put a collar on Sandy by slowly approaching her with treats until she poked her nose through the wide, loosely belted collar, until we could eventually make it fit. She was not used to wearing one inside the house, although we found a nice leather collar and leash inside a closet that Barton probably used when he walked Sandy, before he became ill. The trainer suggested using one of nylon webbing instead, as it would be strong but lighter weight and less bothersome for Sandy.

A few days later Marta found the chewed up collar on the floor. Sandy had a lot of time on her paws and had been gnawing at it since it was sat so low on her neck and she wanted that thing off. She had years of experience chewing off Barton's curtains and books. We decided to use Barton's leather collar after all.

Among other things he taught us about was "go find it", an interactive game on how to throw treats in the opposite direction forcing her to search and work for them. That game would prove to be very valuable, especially when we wanted to distract Sandy from a bad behavior and also in preventing her biting in certain situations.

One day shortly after a session with trainer # 2, we walked across the street to meet his golden retriever, who was waiting outside his car under a shady tree. I made the mistake of kneeling down eye level to pet him because the dog suddenly jumped up and knocked me to the ground and luckily I fell on the grassy sidewalk or I would have had a broken my elbow, but it was just slightly sprained. It happened so fast that Fred and the trainer did not even notice because suddenly his dog was running across the street and into Sandy's house through the front door that was left ajar. They both chased after him, so that Sandy would not freak out, and the trainer was able to stop and get a hold of his dog and take him back to the car.

Marta had reported that she thought Sandy had hurt her paw because she had seen drops of blood on the floor and she was constantly licking her paws.

But on Sunday while visiting with Sandy alone, I noticed blood after she peed so I thought she might have a bladder or kidney infection. I took her to the vet the next day and it turns out Sandy was in heat, which explains why the trainer's male dog frantically tried to get to her.

I could not believe it and I was livid. I told the female vet, that when we first took Sandy for her exam with her friend, trainer #1, the vet tech had told me that she thought Sandy was already spayed. I was very angry at being given this false information, but I was even angrier with Barton for being irresponsible. In this day and age there is no reason not to spay a pet unless they are show dogs and as gorgeous as Sandy was, I knew she was not one.

I asked the vet if she could spay her right then and there, and she just looked at me as if I were crazy. She told me that we had to wait at least a month and I said, "You mean Sandy is going to have her period for a whole month?" I have to admit that in those days I really knew very little about dogs and I had not had one since my childhood dog Estrellita. The vet told us to keep Sandy away from other dogs and I also confirmed with trainer #2 that his dog was neutered so there was no problem.

But perhaps the most useful tip to fit into our lifestyle was learning all about potty training pads even though Sandy was already house trained. I did not even know that they existed because our childhood dog Estrellita grew up in a very large home in Guatemala with lots of land. But because we did not have a yard in our townhouse, getting Sandy outside would become a huge issue. Before Sandy would be making her final move into our townhome, trainer #2 came over to help us figure out where she would be sleeping and eating and he thought the setup I created behind the living room couch with a balcony lined with the pads for her bathroom needs would be perfect. I had told him about the makeshift garden that I had previously created for Sandy and he thought that although it was a great idea, that my problem was a lack of proper drainage and this would be a lot easier and cleaner to mantain.

We felt that these sessions would hold us over while we read more about dog behavior, care and nutrition while adjusting to our lives together.

We called on trainer #3, whose card I found at a former vet's office, when we could not get Sandy down to the foyer and out the front door to the common area so that we could walk her. He referred to himself as a "pet psychologist" who could solve any behavioral issue. I had explained to him on the phone that Sandy had special needs and thought that once he met her in person he was going to be patient and eager to learn about her background, which would shed light on her behavior. Instead he was a very uptight, quirky, neurotic little man who reminded me of Woody Allen. All I could think of during our session was that he could use some therapy himself. Instead of putting the leash on Sandy to take her out for a walking session, maybe I should put it around him and take him for a walk just to loosen him up! What a complete waste of money. We only used him once.

A distant cousin who had dealt with her dog's separation anxiety referred trainer #4 to us. She claimed the woman solved her problem quickly, not realizing that Max at the time was six months old, and a mellower breed, as opposed to Sandy being almost six years. That makes a huge difference because Sandy had so much baggage.

Trainer #4 was also very expensive and we had an intensive two-hour class. She felt that Sandy was the most difficult dog that she had ever worked with because she had so many issues. She used gloves while handling her because she was afraid that Sandy was so distrustful that she would get bitten. My main objective was to get Sandy down stairs without a struggle and the trainer suggested that food motivation was the easiest way for her to respond. I informed her that I tried that but it wasn't working. The best thing this trainer suggested for us was to "up the ante." She said that Sandy's regular food was not going to do the trick. It had to be something special, a different treat, that way she would associate going out with a positive reinforcement and just focus on that. Now instead of being fearful about going out the front door, Sandy's primal instinct would only be concentrating about getting the treat. We used fresh roasted turkey from the deli, low sodium of course, and it worked like a charm. But the trainer also advised us to start asserting ourselves as leaders of the pack, and gave us some helpful tips so that at one point we could get Sandy downstairs without food, because she was afraid that soon Sandy would start demanding filet mignon or lobster!

Once we mastered getting Sandy out the front door without a lot of drama, I still needed help just walking her, so I called on trainer #5 for help.

Trying to walk Sandy on a leash was close to impossible, because she was like a wild mustang, and pulled me and dragged me all over the place. Fred was not capable of handling her in any way, as I already knew from the very beginning. Sandy was too fast, too strong, and she would always end up tangling the leash around him, as if she had lassoed him in. I had to get to a place where it was comfortable for both of us to go outside without a constant struggle and causing us a great deal of anxiety and stress.

I had tried unsuccessfully over a period of time to get several dog walkers to come and help us out, but Sandy never made any effort to acknowledge their presence by going up to smell them, and they felt they could not work with a dog that showed no interest in them and in going outside. Most of their canine clients are happy, friendly dogs, who are waiting by the front door with a leash on their mouths, ready to go out. The various dog walkers did not have the time or energy or patience to try and coax Sandy. After all they are in business and need to walk as many dogs possible in a day. All said to give them a call when she is socialized. And I said to myself "to hell with them." I was so desperate to exercise Sandy that I resorted to running her around the coffee table in the living room and up the few stairs to our dining room, around the dining table and down again, over and over again with a treat dangling from my hand, so she would be motivated to follow me.

With trainer # 5 we had three, also very expensive sessions over three Saturdays at our townhouse, and started with very short walks and stopping as soon as Sandy pulled. Once she did this I would go in the opposite direction and start again. Also what really helped was to make her sit down if she pulled. I was afraid that Sandy would bite me if I tapped and pushed her bottom down as I was instructed to do, but since we were outside in the common area and the trainer was right beside me, it worked. We did drill after drill until it became second nature.

Some of the best advice that trainer #5 gave me was the use of the proper collar and leash for Sandy's temperament. All of the previous trainers had varying opinions on what kind to use. Trainer #1 had suggested using two long leashes tied together so that Sandy would have a lot of space between us, similar to the retractable ones you see people using in the dog parks. This was completely wrong for me to use because that is the easiest way to loose control and get all tangled up. It is also very dangerous. There is a reason for the saying "to keep somebody on a short leash."

At first we experimented with a Martingale collar, which prevents them from backing out and later decided on an English slip lead made of thick, soft, and lightweight but strong silky rope, so that it would not hurt her neck, and it would also prevent her from pulling and backing out, and was much easier to use because it could also be locked at the right point. It keeps Sandy right by my side with enough slack for comfort and easy movement while making her feel safe. It is similar to the kind that most veterinarians use when handling animals in their office and is used as well in most show dogs. Being able to do this boosted my self-confidence as well as Sandy's, and helped us to bond even further together.

Another extremely valuable lesson from trainer #5 was to enlighten me as to the power of play for Sandy as a de-stressor, and for her emotional wellbeing, as well as mental stimulation to prevent boredom.

She noticed that Sandy had tons of toys, and I told her that after playing with them once she would immediately lose interest. But she insisted that I keep on trying and experimenting with different kinds, and that is when I discovered Mr. Googles.

I disagreed with trainer #5 when she suggested that a fun interactive game for Sandy would be "tug-o-war." Knowing that she is a fearful dog I did not want to bring out her aggressive side any further. I did extensive research on the subject and it seems that many different trainers and behaviorists have varying opinions on it. Apparently the human has to win most of the time otherwise the animal will get aggressive. This clearly was not a game for Sandy.

After all these trainers' advice, I used only the tips that would best suit Sandy's personality and temperament, and felt her training at this point was good enough for us all to coexist peacefully. No more trainers!

Fred and I watched many dog training shows on TV hoping to learn as much as we could, and one of my favorites is Victoria Stilwell from Britain. She reminds me of Emma Peel, the iconic English heroine of the 60's TV show "The Avengers." She is beautiful, hip, and tough. And she is always shown driving through the English countryside in her sports car just like Diana Rigg was on her show. Ironically, a few years ago, while working as a costumer on a TV sitcom, I had the pleasure of meeting Patrick Mcknee who was making a guest appearance. He used to play the role of Mr. Steed on "The Avengers", and was as charming in person.

Chapter Seven

GROOMERS

During the time of Barton's illness, we noticed that Sandy's fur was matted all over, as he was just too sick to groom her himself as he had always done. Barton had her dog shampoo, conditioner and brushes all stashed away in the bathroom cabinet, but had not used them in a very long time. Sandy resembled Cinderella before she went to the ball.

Soon after his death, we realized that it was going to be a battle to take Sandy to a grooming salon, where she might have to wait and be surrounded by other animals, and my mom helped me find a mobile groomer in the yellow pages. This was way before the explosion of mobile groomers now saturating the market. They would come to our home in a van equipped with a bathtub and warm water, grooming table, drier and more. I would sit outside the van so that Sandy could see me at all times and not feel abandoned, scared and insecure about having a total stranger handling her. After talking to so many other groomers who sounded impatient, and not too keen about working with Sandy, because she was aggressive when fearful, often making comments like "give me a call when she is trained", these new groomers seemed up to the challenge and appeared to understand her temperament and situation the best.

The first time I met David was when I was recovering from knee surgery at my mom's house, and of course Sandy came to stay with me since I could not bear to be apart from her for very long. My mom agreed to have her stay at her home with the condition that Sandy had to be bathed often, especially since she shed a lot. I was very anxious as to how Sandy would react to him, given that she was so high-strung and fearful, and I was especially worried that she might bite him. But as soon as David walked trough the door he put my mind at ease. I have never met a more confident and mature eighteen year old in my entire life. His good looks resembled a cross between Leonardo DiCaprio and Zac Efron, and he had a leader of the pack attitude. Sandy immediately trusted and respected David and eventually grew to care for him, and demonstrated her affection by shyly wagging her tail when she saw him and knew that he cared for her as well. Along with his fiancé Silvia by his side, they were both so mature for being so young, they groomed Sandy, taking turns in handling her and helped enormously in socializing her.

David and Silvia were Sandy's groomers for about a year and a half until he started getting involved in the martial arts and did not want to give up his Saturday's anymore and Silvia was transferring to a university.

I knew that this day would come because they were both very young and had other interests. However, I learned a lot about dog behavior and care through them and will always be grateful for the kindness they showed Sandy.

Once they were gone, I thought that it was going to be impossible to replace them. I was upset that Sandy would have to get used to somebody else all over again especially when there had been continuity in her life, but sometimes a change can also be good.

As usual, I did a lot of research and called around trying to find the right fit for Sandy's personality, and I was very specific about my requirements for the prospective new groomer. Among other things that I expected was a great deal of patience, gentleness and understanding of Sandy's background. Along came Stacie.

The first time I ever saw her, she appeared to be about fifteen, a very pretty little blonde girl, driving this huge van into our then townhouse driveway. My first thought was "what have they sent me here?" Stacie was as petite as I was and I was afraid she would not be strong enough to carry Sandy, and she also did not exude confidence the way David had.

As Stacie made her way up the stairs into our living room, Sandy barked and barked at her, but Stacie kept calm and sat down on the carpet until Sandy quieted down. She told Fred and I a little bit about herself and that she had recently moved out to

California from Nebraska, and was reassuring us that she has done this before. After about a half an hour later, Stacie says, "Sandy seems relaxed now", and suddenly gets up and scoops her up, carrying her down the flight of stairs into the van, and starts to clip Sandy's toenails! Then lifted her into the bathtub and started lathering her! I was speechless especially because Sandy did not even put up a fight!

Stacie really gave Sandy a major bath, scrubbing her with a special nylon sponge that is used in spas, and gave her a great trim, comb out and blow dry. Afterwards Sandy looked like a princess and seemed to like and trust Stacie who took a great deal of time with her. I appreciated her great patience and efforts so much that I called her boss and told him he had a new client. He was very happy with the good news especially because he had gone out of his way trying to accommodate and help me on a very short notice and it paid off.

Since Sandy has ongoing skin flare-ups because of her allergies and seborrhea, my vet and I discussed the benefits of frequent bathing. At first I was really skeptical about it thinking that it would dry her skin out, but the doctor explained that washing away the allergens more frequently is a common solution for dogs with skin problems and helps to prevent the itching and scratching and discomfort that goes along it. I was willing to try anything that would heal Sandy's skin so I agreed to have her bathed every other week and eventually weekly. I spent countless hours doing research on the proper shampoos and conditioners for her chronic skin condition and experimented with many different kinds, often alternating on a monthly basis because some of the ingredients were medicated. I also decided to buy all of her grooming tools as well, from several online pet supply stores and catalogues, so Sandy would not have to share and possibly contaminate other pets or vice versa.

I kept everything in Sandy's own beauty caddy and she liked having her very own things, which she often examined and smelled with great curiosity. Over a period of time Sandy's skin improved by ninety per cent, due to the baths, home cooked meals and vitamin supplements, especially the fatty acids such as Omega 3 and 6. Sandy was no longer ripping the fur out of her body the way she used to, except on those occasions on which she had an allergy flare-up or insect bite, and then it is managed. For so long it had been excruciating to watch and not being able to help her, because she would get aggressive if we interrupted her chewing, and as a result ended doing herself more damage.

As I got to know Stacie better, I realized how strong she really was when she informed us that she had a 100-pound Saint Bernard that she would carry into her car. We learned she had been a gymnast in school and that she had also worked in a veterinarian's office back in Nebraska. Stacie had come out to LA to pursue acting, and started to do work as an extra on the side, until she got her SAG card. She had a great deal of determination which I admired, and that combined with her all American good looks will take her far in her career.

Stacie was with us for over one year until she felt she needed to move on. I expected that from a twenty one year old, just as I had expected that from Sandy's previous young groomers.

I now knew that I would find somebody else to be compatible with Sandy. I started my search all over again and found Luke.

Luke has a very calm, low-key demeanor much like that of Marta, which was perfect for Sandy and me. We needed someone who was going to be very patient with her and he has proven to be the most patient, dependable and punctual groomer that Sandy has ever had, even though she hasn't always been on her best behavior with him. That is an understatement, yet he really seems to understand and care for her.

Luke is a man of few words in complete contrast to Sandy's constant barking and my energy that has often been described as exuberant. He reminds me of the Marlboro Man, exuding a quality of a loner riding his horse away in the snowy distance. He is the kind of guy that knows how to do everything, and has also helped us do some handyman work around the house. Luke also has a bit of a James Dean quality, is into motorcycles and has the kind of analytical mind that likes to take things apart so he can see how they were put together in the first place. But I am happy he is not a loner like Barton was. I have met his mother, his younger brother and his little niece, and more recently his father who came to visit from Pennsylvania.

Luke was married about a year ago to his childhood sweetheart and is now in his late twenties and ready to settle down.

He has been coming to us every Sunday for almost four years and Sandy has grown very fond of him and rarely acts out against him these days. However when he rings the doorbell Sandy pretends she doesn't know who he is and barks non stop and goes to hide in the bedroom until I tell her "it's Luke, shampoo, shampoo, shampoo." Then I capture her with the leash telling Fred, "I am now in possession of the Sheltie", and take her out the front door until she sees Luke sitting on the steps of his van waiting for her. He always greets us with a "good morning girls". Sandy quietly approaches him, shyly wagging her tail and sniffing him as he gives her treats, and letting herself be petted and scratched. Luke says she is finally acting like a dog.

For a while Sandy has had very cat-like behavior, elusive and aloof, and she constantly grooms herself like a cat, and on occasion even swatting us with her paws like cats do, leading us to believe she had at one point been raised by a cat. I asked Fred if he remembered his Aunt Sally ever having a cat and he believes there was one around when Sandy was a puppy. I told Luke all this and he said, "now I understand, it makes sense, Sandy was raised by a cat."

We moved to our new house shortly after Luke had started with us, and the grooming experience is so much smoother and relaxing because our house is one story and the neighborhood is quiet and peaceful. Sandy doesn't have to deal with cars and people and dogs coming and going through the common area driveway anymore.

Now I get to sit in a lawn chair right under a big lush shady tree in our front yard, while Luke is parked on our front driveway. While Sandy is getting groomed, I watch her and read my Sunday newspaper and enjoy the simple pleasures of life. When it rains I sit inside the van and chat with Luke, and we have had many interesting conversations, as he is not as quiet or reserved as he used to be. Sandy also feels secure by having me nearby and she has grown by leaps and bounds as far as letting herself be handled all over, especially with the nail clipping and ear cleaning, and no longer cowers with the blow-drying.

Having Sandy groomed at home does not come cheap but it has been the best investment towards her health. I would rather spend the money on her wellbeing than on myself for reasons of vanity. I have heard so many horror stories about bad grooming salon experiences when the pets are left unattended. Some of my friend's pets have come home with broken or missing teeth, cuts around the eyes or cheeks and other parts of the skin, and bleeding nails from cutting them to close to the quick. Sometimes it is days before the pet parent notices something is wrong with their animal companions, because unfortunately the animals can't report back what happened to them, and then the groomer or the salon will not take responsibility for its actions because it should have been addressed right away.

In some extreme cases I have heard of dogs coming home with broken legs or dying from strangulation when they are chained by the neck to the grooming table and slip off accidentally. Although it is not an option for a lot of people, I would never drop off my dog and leave it unattended for several hours. To me it is like leaving a child all alone at the mercy of others, in a beauty salon or barbershop, and picking it up many hours later. If I did not have the time to wait around I would rather not do it at all.

Chapter Eight

MR. GOOGLES

When we first met Sandy she had many assorted toys that Barton had bought her, but she was never interested in playing with any of them except for several beach balls in various sizes. She played soccer with them, balancing the ball between both front paws and pushing it with her nose, never missing a beat. It was the cutest thing to watch. I suspect she was herding the ball around pretending it was sheep.

I gave away most of them to the animal shelter nearby so that other homeless dogs would be able to distract themselves and feel that they had something of their own to play with while awaiting their fate. Sandy approved my decision as I put one toy at a time under her nose and said" bye-bye." Only a few times would she stop me with her paw or retrieve it from a box, and we kept those.

My intention was to get Sandy different toys from the kind that she had, as a way of getting her interested in playing more and starting with a clean slate. Every time I bought Sandy a new toy she would initially show some excitement and bark non-stop. When I would take it out of the bag she could hardly wait for me to tear off the packaging so she could take it away from me and run away to her "den." But after only a few minutes with her "prey," she was bored and done with it. Because we did not have a yard, Sandy had no place to bury her toys as dogs normally do, and she would run back and forth restlessly with the toy in her mouth in complete frustration, so I laid out towels or blankets throughout our living room floor so she could dig and hide her valued possessions.

Without realizing it, my new hobby soon became searching for the right toy that would capture Sandy's imagination. I spent countless hours on a weekly basis going to pet supply shops going through the aisles and eventually was on a first name basis with the entire staff that tried to help me. They would always ask me about how Sandy was doing and told me to bring the toy back if she did not like it. As a result I became such a loyal customer that I gave them great business. Aside from shopping in stores I started buying on-line and discovered the never-ending world of dog toys and supplies available these days. It is truly mind-boggling. In the olden days with my childhood dog Estrellita, a simple ball, biscuit or chew toy would suffice.

I felt that Sandy really did not have it in her to play since I had tried so many toys for so long. But the last trainer that Sandy had, taught me the importance of playtime, especially for a fearful and high-strung dog like her. It would also help to prevent destructive behavior and would help Sandy to get in touch with her canine instincts. I took her advice and kept on trying until I hit the jackpot.

When I came across Mr. Googles, a goofy looking and colorful latex turkey leg drumstick with a funny face and big smile, it would prove to be a defining moment in Sandy's life. What made him so special was that he was a squeaky toy. I guess Sandy had never had one of those before, because as soon as I took him out of the bag she was fascinated with him. At first she frenetically smelled him then sat down with a puzzled look on her face and later, slowly and suspiciously, approached him and swatted him with her paw and ran away. She barked and barked at him hysterically with a very high pitched voice and started scratching the carpet, running to and fro, and circling around him until she finally had built up her confidence, and took Mr. Googles in her mouth and squeaked him non-stop until she wore herself out. I had never seen anything like it or Sandy react that way to a toy before, it was quite a spectacle. She was officially in play mode!

At bedtime I took the toy away, surprisingly without any problem. I had anticipated a possessive attitude from Sandy, but pretended to put Mr. Googles to sleep and gave her a treat for being a good girl. It became the thing to do each evening after dinner because I did not want to leave Sandy unattended with the toy. The instructions on the package were very specific and even though Fred was home during the day, he could not watch her 24/7. My instincts were dead on, because within two days she had chewed holes into it and was close to biting off and possibly swallowing the squeaker, which was a chocking hazard. I tried to replace it immediately but could not find another one just like it anywhere, so I bought her another latex squeaky toy that was more of a fetch toy and she loved it as well. Sandy soon associated every toy that had a squeaker as Mr. Googles. When I would ask her "where is Mr. Googles?" she would run over to her toy box which was up high on the bookshelf and bark until I took him down. She is very, very smart.

Mr. Googles changed Sandy's life by making her more playful and relaxed and especially more confident. As time went on she was definitely less destructive and that paved the way for other toys that would bring out her predatory instincts in a safe manner. The realistic looking stuffing-free furry wild animals, elicited a completely different response altogether. Sandy would shake and shake the toy while running around with it in her mouth in a madcap race across our living room. It was hysterically funny. All that novelty would bring her about full circle and gave her a chance to exercise indoors and promoted a sense of well being and balance. Her interactive toys are also great for fighting boredom and provide her with the mental simulation that she needed, and as a result she is a much happier dog.

Chapter Nine

THE BATTLE OF VICTORY AND DE SOTO

During a visit to one of Sandy's former vets, the doctor had a sudden emergency and was running behind. As a result the waiting room was full and there was no place to sit, so I decided to wait outside in the car, with all doors opened and with the air conditioner running full blast for a few minutes. But it was so hot even with the air conditioning going on, and it is never a good idea to sit inside a car that is not moving, not even for a short time, especially with a dog inside, that we moved outside and sat on the ledge of a planter in the shade.

I had made such a big effort getting Sandy down the stairs and into the car that instead of going back home and coming back another day we decided to wait. Besides she had a "hot spot" and it needed to be taken care of right away because Sandy was constantly scratching and chewing on herself and I did not want it to get further infected and I knew that she needed antibiotics.

After a long wait, a vet technician startled us by suddenly coming out of the side door nearby, and Sandy got scared and pulled her leash with such force as she panicked, that she managed to back out of her old collar, before the Martingale, and started running loose around the parking lot. I immediately ran after Sandy trying to catch her but she was running so fast I could not get to her. Just a few months before I had had knee surgery and my leg was not strong enough for me to run. I then tripped and fell face down and slid to the ground on the rough and uneven pavement, that if I hadn't been wearing gloves I would have skinned the palms of my hands. It was a miracle that I did not break any of my bones and only had scrapes and minor cuts. In the meantime the female vet tech ran inside the clinic to get a sliding leash and quickly ran back out to the street as I limped inside screaming for more help.

Sandy started to run into the street making her way into the busy intersection and I was hysterically crying and screaming for help. I felt so helpless and thought I was going to lose her forever. I stepped out into the middle of the street waving my arms, making the cars stop. There must have been over fifty cars at the moment.

Traffic on all four sides of the intersection came to a complete standstill as people were stopping and getting out of their cars to help me out.

One man driving a convertible jeep stopped and jumped out of his car and attempted to catch and carry Sandy as she was running back and forth in a very agitated state, between all the cars and people who were trying to block her. Sandy was putting up a good fight, although he almost got her, but she wrangled out of his arms as she was biting him.

I apologized and offered to get him some medical care, but he said for me not to worry and just drove away. I did not even have the chance to thank him or learn his name. I am now convinced that he was a guardian angel, because nobody else seemed to notice him even being there.

Soon after, two very athletic and strong young male vet technicians came out running into the street with more sliding leashes and blankets and tried to corner Sandy.

I was truly moved by all the strangers' efforts to help me with Sandy and it restored my faith in humanity if only for a while.

At exactly 3:04 PM, on that unforgettable Saturday afternoon, the spirited Sheltie surrendered herself and was captured at the corner of Victory and De Soto.

I never went back to that clinic again.

Chapter Ten

ONE OF THE WORST DAYS OF OUR LIVES

With tragic foresight one of our worst fears came true. Several renters moved into a unit across from our townhouse. There was something very unsavory about these people and soon all our neighbors were feeling very uncomfortable because these tenants were extremely noisy, and had parties all the time, even on weekdays till the wee hours of the morning. People parked in front of their door in the common area driveway, blocking others cars and they had no regard for other neighbors and felt that the rules we all lived under, did not apply to them. But the biggest problem was their dog, a pit bull, which by their own admission was very aggressive especially to other animals. Yet they let this powerhouse of an animal roam loose, unleashed, in the common area where smaller dogs and children played, and even let him swim in the common pool with a feeling of entitlement, not caring about the safety and health risks to others. All the neighbors were afraid, yet ignored our cry for help when we tried to have the homeowners association as well as the management company enforce the townhouse rules. An animal like that, through no fault of their own, in the hands of the wrong people is as good as a lethal weapon.

Fred and I had sent numerous e-mails to the board and all the residents warning them of the potential for disaster in a situation like this. It was also discussed at various association meetings and still nothing was done until it was too late.

I had hired Sandy's groomer, who was also a dog walker to help me out with Sandy after I had knee surgery, and we always walked inside the gates in the common area where we thought we were safe. That fateful evening as the three of us walked around a cluster of townhomes we noticed that the pit bull was hanging outside his living room window, because the screen was missing, and he looked as if he was ready to jump out. We quickly left the area and I told the walker to go in the far opposite direction with Sandy while I went to talk to the renter. When I knocked on the door, I immediately stepped back into the middle of the common area so they could see me from the upstairs balcony where they were always hanging around. Unexpectedly, the door was opened by another careless roommate of theirs and in a split second, the pit bull bolted out charging into the far end of the common area where Sandy and her walker, a young, athletic and very fit twenty three year old girl were, and knocked them both to the ground.

As I watched in horror, in a slow motion kind of way, I heard Sandy's blood curdling screams as the pit bull was brutally attacking her. For a moment I felt as if I were paralyzed, I simply could not move, and all of a sudden I started to run towards them, almost as if in a trance, as if I were floating.

I was in complete shock during this surrealistic moment. Everything around me was a blur, as I was in the middle of a living nightmare. All I could hear was my heart beating so fast and my feet pounding on the pavement. I was completely out of breath that I thought I was going to pass out.

With all of my might, I grabbed the pit bull by his collar on the backside of his neck, and dragged him away from Sandy who was bleeding profusely and was trembling and in shock. The dog walker, who was not hurt, and Sandy quickly ran inside the house leaving a trail of blood.

Now I can understand when you hear these stories in the news about women who can lift a car in order to save their babies. I don't know how I was physically able with my ever-frail frame, to remove the aggressive beast that weighed more than I do, away from Sandy.

Aside from that, the pit bull could have turned around and killed me in an instant. Later, all I kept thinking about was the infamous case about the San Francisco woman, who was savagely killed by the vicious Presa Canario dogs in her apartment hallway. Nobody had come to her aid despite her cries for help.

The owner of the pit bull, whom I can only describe as déclassé, was the live in girlfriend of the tenant. He himself had admitted to being afraid of the dog. The woman finally came down when she heard all the commotion while the neighbors were gathering around, and told me to take my hands of her dog. She did not apologize for what had happened, and had no remorse, saying that Sandy had provoked her dog and it was her own fault that she got attacked. I warned her that if she did not do the right thing she was going to end up in jail.

Fred was upstairs when all of this happened, but immediately ran down when he suddenly heard Sandy screaming in pain, unawares of what had just taken place, and immediately called the police when he found out. We were connected to animal control as we both waited on the phone, but they were unable to come right away because of a backlog of calls. In the meantime, Animal Control took a phone report from the dog walker, as well as neighbors who were witnesses and later us, and said they would come out and investigate but could not give us a time or day.

In the meantime the dog walker put a towel around an injured Sandy and gently carried her into her car and drove us to the Animal Emergency Hospital, which is open twenty-four hours a day. We had already alerted them that we were on our way, and they immediately gave Sandy an antibiotic injection as soon as we arrived. The female veterinarian took ex-rays to make sure no bones were broken and informed us that Sandy had several deep puncture wounds and lacerations, and the only thing that they could do at the time is to staple her. That is now being done instead of stitches. Normally they will not operate unless it is absolutely necessary, but she warned us that the area where Sandy was injured the most, the groin, was very susceptible to bacterial infections because it was a high movement area, and sometimes surgery might be needed after all.

Sandy was trembling and in shock, so they did not even give her a strong sedative as this was being done. She was sent home with a slew of medications and painkillers, and I was told to keep Sandy in a confined area to restrict her movement, and to keep things very quiet and calm around her.

When we got home, I tried several times to give Sandy her medication with a piece of turkey wrapped around it, which in a normal situation she would have gulped down, instead she would turn her face away, and was disoriented and shaking. Fighting back my tears, I just lied next to her on the carpet behind the couch, and put a baby gate to block the area off. I put a plastic liner underneath her blanket to prevent the blood from seeping through, but Sandy decided to sleep out in her balcony instead, on her potty pads. She is an unbelievably clean doggie and instinctively knew she would get her bed dirty. It was summer and still very warm outside.

Fred and I skipped dinner that night. I never left Sandy's side for two weeks, except to take a quick shower, sleeping beside her on the carpet, and hand feeding her as if she were a little sparrow. I took time off from work without pay because I had already used my vacation time.

The next day after Sandy's attack, I called another vet she had seen previously, who also made house calls. He came over and checked her out, and said that everything seemed to be in order and for me to look out for other warning signals of pain and discomfort. I did extensive research on all her medications, so that I would be able to immediately identify any side effects.

Sandy could hardly move and she wasn't going to the bathroom and the doctor told me that animals are very resilient and that we need to give them more credit, and that slowly she would get back to her normal body functions. He also emphasized that I should not baby or show pity towards Sandy because she would pick up on the negative feelings and that would not be good for her recovery. I finally was able to give Sandy her pills with a little lump of her canned pumpkin and she finally dozed off for a bit.

I was shaken, exhausted, feeling dazed and extremely guilty, and blamed myself for what had happened to her, constantly re-living the incident in my mind. I kept on thinking that if I had not knocked on that door Sandy would be okay. Neighbors and friends tried to comfort and reassure me by saying that it would of happened sooner or later, given the closeness of the homes, and the careless attitude of the bad neighbors. Although I have tried to make peace with it, a part of me will never forgive myself. Guilt is a terrible thing. It is one of the cruelest of punishments.

I did not sleep at all that night and could not wait till daytime so that I could call animal control again. The officer on the phone said that they take these things very seriously and that I just had to be patient until they could come out. He urged me to take photos of her injuries, which would prove to be helpful in prosecuting the case.

In the meantime Fred and I called the management company to report Sandy's attack and urged the board to do something about it, but nobody wanted to take any responsibility.

I demanded the phone number of the homeowner who rented the unit to those derelicts and kept on bugging them until they finally gave it to me. I then called the homeowner and he pretended that he did not know his renters had a dog, much less a pit bull. I told him that I had all the e-mails communicating my fears to the management company as well as the homeowners association and that he needed to evict those people. I also told him that his insurance company should reimburse me for the vet bills and he had the gall to say he did not have homeowners insurance. That got me angry. Nobody wanted to be held accountable, but I was not about to let it go. It is just not in my nature.

After a few days I thought Sandy was getting better because of all the medications she was on, and was told that I could lift the baby gate periodically so that she could start moving around and stretching her muscles more. I put out towels throughout our living room carpet so that Sandy could lie on them, but noticed a large bright red spot on the beige carpet thinking that Fred had spilled some cranberry juice, and when I got up close to clean it up my heart sank, and I felt a wave of nausea come over me, they way people feel when they get bad news. It was fresh blood, still warm. Sandy was bleeding again, and was vocalizing her pain throughout the next two nights. I immediately called the vet's exchange because it was late Saturday night. He told me to bring her in first thing on Monday morning to his office to see another doctor because he was going to be on Jury duty, and that most likely she would need to be operated on. When I called, all the other vets were booked, and I was told to drop her off and they would see her in between. I pleaded with them saying this was an emergency and I was not about to leave her alone to be seen in four hours or so. Fred and I started frantically searching for other veterinarians that could take her in and were also qualified and equipped to perform surgery, and I finally found Dr. Mark Rigoni of the Southern California Veterinary Hospital in Woodland Hills.

I made arrangements the night before with David, her groomer at the time, to use him as a pet taxi the following morning. He came upstairs and very gently wrapped Sandy in a blanket and carried her into the van while his fiancé drove to the hospital. As soon as Sandy arrived they put her on a stretcher and gave her an IV. They needed the inflammation and infection to go down before her surgery. The next morning Sandy had major surgery, because gangrene had set in about the size of a pancake in the groin-abdominal area where she had been bitten, and the tissue was quickly dying. Dr. Rigoni had to perform a skin graft and remove part of her mammary glands. He is a very fine surgeon with a gentle, kind and calm demeanor, and he saved my little girl's life.

Sandy stayed at the hospital for several days and had plugs all over half of her shaven body to drain out the pus. We went to visit her many times throughout the day and brought Sandy her own food because she refused to eat the hospital kind, but when I fed her, she gobbled up her meal. That's my little girl!

At a homeowner's association meeting shortly after Sandy's attack, people kept on minimizing what had happened to her, because she is a dog and not a human. Even after I said, "give me a call when somebody's child ends up in the pit bull's mouth." I admit that was a bit brutal, still my harsh words seemed to bear no weight.

It was obvious that nothing was going to be resolved any time soon, so we paid good money to have a lawyer draft a letter, basically threatening to sue the homeowners association for negligence and endangering our lives. All townhouses would also be assessed. Interesting, that until something has to do with "out of pocket money," then they heard us loud and clear.

The Board, Management Company and the other homeowners finally put pressure on the townhouse owner to evict the bad tenants, and they were forced out within a month, after being given a legal eviction notice by the sheriff. The townhouse owner learned a very hard lesson. Because he had been so desperate to rent out this particular unit, one of many other properties that he owned, he failed to do a complete background check on these people and eventually his renters trashed his place and left owing him several months of rent, costing him much more in the long run. He thought that just because the tenant was good looking and well dressed and a smooth talker, that it was good enough. People like that are also called "con-people."

I called the owner of the townhouse day and night for six months, until I wore him down, and forced him to finally do the right thing. Anybody who knows me well, knows that I am relentless in pursuing justice, until I have exhausted all my possibilities and in the process exhaust the other parties involved. I believe that my tenacity, when it comes to getting restitution especially for Sandy, is a force of nature and my ability to drive people crazy in certain situations, is a God given talent. Over the years I have come to accept the fact that we seldom get to right a wrong, but that has never prevented me from trying.

Sandy had racked up close to $6,000.00 in veterinary bills that I had put on my credit card, and I was reimbursed half by her pet insurance, and finally the other half by the landlord's homeowner's insurance.

I don't agree with the old saying "time heals all wounds" because it simply doesn't. The emotional or physical scars it leaves behind, serve as a reminder and a warning that if we forget what happened, it could happen again.

The fur on that part of Sandy's body where the wounds occurred will never grow in completely due to the scar tissue, and her spirit has healed slowly over the years, still very fearful once we go out the front door, any door.

One of the animal control officers finally came to talk to the woman who owned the aggressive pit bull, but she refused to open the front door. I came down to meet him and told him that she was home because I could see her through our kitchen window. The officer then went around in his truck and climbed over the fence and he could clearly see her standing in her living room. He informed me that her evading the authorities was not going to help her, as he documented everything, and was determined to catch her. A few days later he made another surprise attempt to talk to her and gave her a citation for not having the dog registered and without a current rabies vaccine.

A few weeks later I noticed the woman was packing up and getting ready to skip town without ever dealing with Sandy's attack and the aftermath. I called animal control again and urged them to come out and make her accountable and asked them if this was it, does she get to walk away untouched? They reassured me that they were handling the situation and that she would not get away with it, that they would come unannounced as to not alert her. For the time being I decided to take several photos of her car and a close up of her license plate incase she disappeared, and that way they could track her down easier.

On the last Sunday morning before the woman was to move out completely, Fred spotted an animal control officer at her door, through our kitchen window. With a great deal of excitement he said, "Sand, you are not going to believe this!" "Get over here fast!" "Now, before it's too late!"

"What is it Fred?" "What happened?" "Where are you?"

"In the kitchen, they came to get the dog, they brought the long stick to restrain him!"

I flew down the stairs and watched all the action with the animal control officer through the second story window. Fred and I were glued to the window. Pretty soon another officer, a female, joined him. The pit bull owner refused to open her door so they called for back up and soon after three police officers in black and white cars showed up. This was something out of a TV show.

One of the police officers said, "look lady, I am not going to stand outside all day and I sure as heck am not in the mood to get sunburned, so either you surrender the dog or you will be arrested."

I loved these guys!

The dog was taken into custody and held for ninety days until the hearing with the animal control commissioner.

I owe everything to these officers who came through for me, especially the one woman from animal control, whose name I will not mention in order to protect her identity. I wrote a letter commending this dedicated officer who took her job seriously, and hoped there are more people like her in the world.

She was on a mission when she saw the graphic pictures of Sandy's wounds. At one point she remembered that she had previously had contact with the pit bull's owner on a different occasion, and tirelessly searched through piles of records until she discovered that this particular animal had attacked two other dogs in the past.

On one occasion the pit bull had jumped out of the woman's car while she was driving, because the windows were all rolled down, and attacked a dog that was tethered in his front yard while his owner, an old lady, was gardening. The other incident happened while the dog was let loose to run unleashed in a park, knowing he was not animal friendly.

The officer had given this woman previous warnings, and told her to provide barriers for the aggressive dog, but the woman kept on ignoring and disobeying the law.

I asked another animal control officer again if the pit bull's owner gets to walk away as if nothing had happened, and he promised me that for every day the dog is in their custody and in quarantine, she has to pay a fee for his boarding and food not to mention the cost of involving five officers. It was not going to be cheap.

During the hearing with the animal control commissioner, we were asked if we wanted to have the pit bull put down and we both said no. Fred and I didn't have the heart to do it, and felt that the dog deserved another chance with a more responsible owner. He only did what he was taught to do and we wanted the dog to know what it was like to be happy, if only for a while. We forgave the dog but we never forgave the woman. The commissioner followed our wishes.

It has taken me a long time to get over my deep-seated fear against pit bulls, which started while working on location on a film in East LA many years ago. There was a loose pit bull wondering the streets in a very agitated state, and we were all instructed to stand still and not make any eye contact until the animal control officer came. At the very same time, a lady across the street took out her small, white fluffy puppy to pee in her white picket fence enclosed front yard, and in a split second the pit bull flew across the street, jumped over the fence, and grabbed the playful doggie by the neck killing him in an instant. The poor woman was in shock, horrified, heartbroken, screaming, wailing and crying, holding and cuddling and rocking her dead puppy in her arms. It was a very traumatic incident for all and shortly after the entire crew was released for the day.

I know that there are really no bad dogs or other animals, only bad people, who victimize these poor voiceless animals turning them into walking time bombs, using them as weapons, for their own perverse pleasure and an even more deranged sense of empowerment, engaging them in fights and betting on them to produce quick easy cash, only to be discarded when they have served their purpose and are no longer useful.

I will not go into detail about my feelings regarding a notorious athlete or the ex-husband of a beloved actress, and others who already have very successful careers, money and fame, and yet were and still are involved in merciless dog fighting rings, or I will never finish this book. It is beyond my comprehension why these people have a void in their lives that can never be filled no matter how much they have.

Unfortunately there is a cultural affiliation with these illegal activities and the people involved fail to see how barbaric these practices are exposing young children to witness the abuse and desensitizing them in the process. Some of these children will grow up to be the criminals of tomorrow. It is the same situation with cockfighting or any "sport" where innocent animals are forced into submission and aggression for profit.

It is tragic that these poor animals are guilty by association and that there is a stigma attached to them because gangs have used them over the years to intimidate others.

Only with education, compassion, understanding and respect for all living things, can the cycle of abuse ever be broken.

Fortunately there are many rescue groups willing to take a chance on these unwilling victims and rehabilitate them and eventually place them into loving homes. Hopefully they can reach out to more people and create change in the lives of this very controversial and misunderstood breed.

What happened to Sandy has had a very profound impact on me, and as a result I have turned into quite the animal activist. I am a member of many animal help organizations as well as a volunteer, and spend a great deal of my time writing letters to congressmen, governors, mayors, as well as to our president on behalf of animal welfare. By taking action and signing petitions, and boycotting inhumane products, we can create a positive change on behalf of all sorts of neglected and abused animals who have no voice and are living in deplorable conditions such as farm animals and victims of puppy mills, among others. Helping to pass laws to enforce humane treatment of animals will ultimately get them the justice they deserve, by having their abusers prosecuted.

One of my favorite quotes from Mahatma Gandhi, which is also popular with many animal welfare organizations is: "The greatness of a nation and its moral progress can be judged by the way its animals are treated."

Chapter Eleven

TWO FOR THE PRICE OF ONE?

In what would become a series of surgeries over the years, between Sandy "the human" and Sandy "the Sheltie", they provided the perfect opportunity for us to bond even further as roommates.

When I had knee surgery due to a popiteal cyst I stayed in the hospital overnight and came home with a leg brace and crutches. It was extremely painful especially because my leg was suspended at a halfway point to ensure that I would not rip the stitches in the back of the knee. When I came home, Sandy would not stop barking at my crutches and even tried to bite them. She considered them the enemy and was fighting them just like "Don Quixote" was fighting the windmills in one of my favorite books of all time.

We both stayed at my mom's house for several months during my recovery because I could not go up the steps of our townhome and her home has a downstairs bedroom suite. Sandy took it upon herself to be my private nurse and worked a double shift being my very own bodyguard, watching my every move making sure everything was okay. This also brought about Sandy's compassionate side, which was quite remarkable. She would become anxious and sad when I expressed pain, and would gently put her paw on my other knee or lightly nudge my hand with her nose while looking at me intensely as if to say, "is there anything I can do for you to make you feel better?" or she'd lay her head on my lap in solidarity to commiserate and console me. My pain was her pain.

It made me laugh when I would take a little too long to brush my teeth because I could not balance myself over the sink with the crutches, and Sandy would come and go every couple of minutes to see if I was done, and finally let out a long sigh and settled down once she had lost her patience with me. But the thing that most warmed up my heart, was whenever I took a long shower while sitting on a bath chair that we got from a medical supply store, and Sandy would guard the door and I could see her long fur sliding underneath. It was unbelievably sweet.

During the time that I had another surgery for a fibroid tumor, Sandy was due to finally be spayed at seven years of age. Whenever I had made several attempts to have that done in the past, it was never the right time, for medical reasons according to the vets. This time seemed like the perfect opportunity. I arranged it so that it would be done two weeks after mine, so that we could both heal and recover together once again at my mom's house.

The surgeries were somewhat similar in nature, although Sandy's was more delicate because she actually had a hysterectomy and I did not. Being facetious, I joked with her vet that we both could have had a special, "two for the price of one", deal.

We loved staying with my mom because she has a large backyard where Sandy could safely run free and explore the garden without a leash and without being afraid, or she could just sit on the patio and get some sun and fresh air and wait for a squirrel to shake things up. Not having to climb up all those stairs made things so much easier for both of us. I felt as if I were twelve again, with not a care in the world except to get better, eat as much as I could to put back the weight I had lost, and watch some TV and read magazines while we both healed. Fred was very lonely without us both but would come to see us several times a day between his radio shows everyday, and spend as much time with us as he could. Luckily for us, that my mom's house is only fifteen minutes away from ours.

Chapter Twelve

HOMECOOKING

In an effort to relieve Sandy's ongoing recurrent skin allergies, the main one being seborrhea which causes her to itch, scratch and chew on her fur and paws until raw, as well as constantly scratch her ears, I decided that it would be best if I home cooked all of her meals. This would help to prevent the onset of secondary bacterial infections that require a vicious cycle of antihistamines, antibiotics, cortisones, prednisone and cyclosporine.

Even though I had tried several elimination diets over a period of time while using only premium dog food, and avoiding known allergens such as corn, wheat, soy, and dairy, it was still very hard to pinpoint exactly what she is allergic to, especially because it is also atopic which includes airborne allergens, and I did not want her on any more medication which has terrible side effects over a period of time, as most do.

I discussed this with her vet, Dr. Rigoni, and came up with a plan that would limit one source of protein and one carbohydrate starch and vegetable, to start with for several months until we could see a difference. This way we could keep track of any changes. Since home cooking does not contain all the required nutrients that dogs need, Dr. Rigoni suggested that I supplement her meals with a combination of specially formulated canine vitamins, minerals, digestive enzymes and essential fatty acids with omega 3 and 6 which is found in salmon oil. I did extensive research, as I do with anything regarding Sandy, and experimented with different fish oils and supplements until I was able to find just the right ones for her. In addition, I now give Sandy a digestive supplement containing acidophilus, in a non-dairy cranberry and papaya juice, once a day mixed into her food. This provides her with the antioxidants and probiotics found in yogurt, to help counteract cumulative damage from antibiotics and other medications, and to keep her urinary tract healthy. As Sandy is getting older, I also started using a low dose single source glucosamine for healthy joints and tissue, and that way she can be covered across the board.

As I began my home cooked meals experiment, at first I decided to try ground lamb because it is an easy protein to digest and is considered hypoallergenic. I mixed it with mashed baked potato and grated zucchini to make it into a meat loaf enough for one week. As it was baking, the aroma also proved irresistible to Fred, leading him to ask me what we were having for dinner. He was very disappointed when I told him that it was for Sandy, but since it was premium human grade food he was welcome to have some. Fred realized where he stood in the pecking order of the Wallin household, but was a good sport about it.

For both of us, Sandy is the number one priority.

It didn't take long for people to find out how well I treated Sandy and pretty soon I was getting comments such as "I wish I were your dog", which I consider to be the highest of compliments, or "I know who to leave my children with in case anything happens to me."

Before I realized it, over a period of time Sandy started slowly gaining weight until I finally noticed, and Dr. Rigoni confirmed that she was very overweight. Mea culpa. Pets don't gain weight by themselves. It is always the human's fault unless there is a medical problem. These days pet obesity is directly linked to pet parents and is a result of being a pampered pet, just as much as the epidemic of childhood obesity. I should have drained the fat from the lamb and boiled it instead of sautéing. It took me awhile to fine tune the right food portions as well as the proper proportions of protein and carbohydrates. Even though I had some guidelines it was all very experimental because of Sandy's age, metabolism and level of exercise.

When lamb was not available, I would substitute ground turkey or chicken. Then one day after Sandy had some digestive problems due to eating some raw vegetables that I had been giving to her as a new snack, I started cooking a bland diet of lean skinless and boneless chicken breast boiled with some carrots and zucchini and eventually added tomato and celery making a nice broth without any salt. This has now become her regular food and she loves it. It is also a lot easier for me to make and takes me less time. Sandy is on her very best behavior when I am preparing a fresh pot of chicken soup, quietly supervising me while sitting next to the stove and hoping for a morsel to come her way before her actual meal. When I ask Sandy if she wants chicken soup she goes crazy with excitement and starts twirling around me. It was the only way I could get her to drink more liquids when she started to refuse water. I make her a fresh batch about once a week.

Since everything was going so well, I decided to also make Sandy her dog biscuits with limited ingredients, since so many out there have additional vitamins which were no longer necessary, and over-supplementation can be dangerous.

No meal is complete without an after dinner doggie mint treat. After trying various edible dental chews, I discovered a really great one that is wheat free, completely digestible, low fat and that is good for dogs of all ages and for allergies. It also has parsley, chlorophyll, and mint and gets rid of tartar and plaque and has given Sandy the whitest teeth and the freshest breath of anybody that I ever met. Dr. Rigoni says her teeth are in terrific shape for a dog her age, that she has not needed cleaning in over two years. My little girl lives for this treat. Every night at exactly eight p.m. sharp, because Sandy is very punctual, she waits in anticipation for her doggie mint in the same spot. If I happen to be a little bit late in giving it to her, she starts glaring at me from far away or comes looking for me and scolds me or makes a big scandal until I give it to her. Then she has some soup to wash it down and takes a long nap before bedtime.

With the decrease in food portions one spoonful at a time, and the increase of activity, although it has taken a long time, I was finally able to stabilize her weight, and Sandy has regained her girlish figure.

Over a period of time I saw a drastic improvement in her skin and coat and weaned her off all medications, only using them if absolutely necessary when she has bad flare-ups. The combination of her special diet, supplements, exercise, playtime, and weekly baths to remove the airborne allergens, especially pollen from her fur, has made a monumental difference in her life, health and attitude. It takes a lot of work, commitment and consistency, but it is also very rewarding. All the elements combined together have created a more healthy, happy and balanced dog with a lush gleaming coat and younger appearance.

Chapter Thirteen

RANTING, RAVING AND PET PEEVES

One of my biggest pet peeves is when people take any doctors', veterinarians', dentists', or lawyers' opinion as gospel. They give these people way too much power, not knowing that they as well, often err. If I have learned anything at all over the years is that it is important to take matters into our hands and take charge of our own lives and the lives of those we care about, especially our beloved animal companions, which rely completely on us. It is crucial to get second and third or even more opinions as well as doing our very own research, so that we can be informed and help these professionals help us, with the proper questions. I have often questioned figures of authority, who consider themselves experts, making me somewhat a bit of a pain in the neck, and if they are the slightest offended at my lack of faith, so be it. To me it indicates a certain level of arrogance on their part. My intention is not to challenge them but to get the right answers.

The reason I am bringing this up is mainly because as pet parents it is our obligation and responsibility to properly care for our voiceless animals. Unlike children who learn to voice their discomfort or pain, we often don't realize our pets are sick until the situation is critical and in some cases too late.

When we finally moved to our new home with the big backyard that we longed to give Sandy for so long, I saw an increase in her ear infections. She would itch, scratch, rub and shake her ears and I realized it was due to the fact that now she came in direct contact with more allergens, not just in the grass and flowers but also in the air. To begin with, her immune system had been compromised, as is the case with any animal or person that suffers from allergies. This was sort of a "catch 22" situation, a damn if you do and damn if you don't.

The fact that Sandy was constantly licking and chewing her paws would then bring the culprits that she picked up from the soil directly into her ear as she scratched, creating a moist environment where bacteria would flourish.

I took Sandy to the nearby vet and he ordered a smear and stain of her ear to find out if the infection was of the bacterial or viral nature so he would know how to treat it. In the meantime he prescribed broad-spectrum drops, but the problem was that it was not getting down to the ear canal, because the ear was so inflamed. The vet technicians, who administered the meds daily because Sandy would not let me do so, did not inform me, or the doctor, that her ears were not getting better. When the vet got the lab results back, he ordered a culture to determine exactly what kind of bacteria it was, and that would take another two weeks because it has to grow separately in a petri dish.

By the time the diagnosis was complete even though I had been diligent with the treatment and with follow ups, Sandy was exhibiting signs of vestibular illness. That is when the dog walks around and around in circles, disoriented because of the loss of equilibrium, and cocking its head to the sides in pain. We tried another medication when as it turned out she had a staff infection, which is extremely hard to cure, and in some cases can be fatal. When the new medication was still not working, Sandy's groomer Luke suggested I get a second opinion, so I took her back to Dr. Rigoni. It was well worth the long trip. He said that although the eardrops were adequate, the severe inflammation prevented her cure and her eardrum had been punctured. He prescribed Prednisone, as well as oral antibiotics to aggressively treat it, and within a few days there was a vast improvement and eventual cure.

The fact that Sandy had had the infection for several months made me very angry. I blame this kind of situation on the lack of communication between doctors and their staff. There was no need for Sandy to suffer for so long without a solution. But Sandy's case is one that I hear about over and over again, and in some cases the poor dog will need surgery. The ear is very, very delicate and any slight infection should be taken seriously and addressed right away.

After spending so much money on Sandy's ear infections, especially since her pet insurance had excluded coverage for such treatment permanently, I started to do a lot of research on natural cures and ways to prevent future infections or at least to nip them in the bud. To my surprise one of the most effective preventatives on recurring ear infections is also one of the least expensive. A homemade solution of warm water and white vinegar mixed in a bottle with a dropper. It restores the ph balance in the ear and makes it impossible for bacteria to survive. In the cases of staff infections, apparently tea tree oil is very effective, and I discovered some over the counter ear wash and dry solution to be used together. Once we started using this combo on Sandy's ears twice weekly, thus preventing moisture from forming inside her ear canal, which is usually the cause of the problem, she has not had an ear infection again.

Then there was the case of the tapeworms. I was shocked to see what looked like moving grains of white rice in Sandy's stool as I was picking up after her, especially since I had never seen that before. I quickly put the sample in between two paper plates and wrapped it in a plastic bag and labeled it. Soon after I dropped it off to the nearby vet, and told the woman at the front desk that there were mini worms that were moving and she said they would take care of it and send it out to the lab. A couple of days later the results came back negative for parasites. I could not believe it so I did my own research. I was very upset because the test the lab had performed was a flotation one and it was the wrong kind.

Again, I told the same woman that it was not possible since I saw living, moving worms, and she said to bring in another sample. Talking about inconvenience and a waste of my time, and the unnecessary need to prolong Sandy's condition. This time I made double sure that several people, especially the vet technicians, see the sample as I personally opened the package in front of them. They agreed that it was tapeworms and that Sandy would need several rounds of de-worming. I made sure that they were not going to charge me for the second test, as the woman had taken it upon herself to determine what kind the lab should do, without consulting the vet.

I did not want to get her in trouble because she was very nice, but things like these just cannot happen, especially since it could have adverse effects on the patient if left untreated over a period of time. Once again, this is due to lack of communication and improper training of the staff. I then wished that I had seen my former vet instead, but figured something like this was so basic and I was not able to make the far trip to his office at the time. Another lesson that I learned is that not only do I have to do my job but I also have to stay on top of others to do theirs!

I also found out that some tapeworms are zoonotic and can be transmitted to humans. If left untreated the tapeworms start eating the lining of the intestinal wall and spread to other organs and over a period of time can be even fatal. It surprised me to find out how tapeworms are transmitted. In most cases it comes from an infected flea that is ingested by the dog through licking it's skin during a fleabite or from contaminated soil. I was very puzzled by this because according to various vets and groomers they have not found any fleas on Sandy and she is on a preventative as well for her protection. Also Sandy has had little contact with other dogs except on her visits to the vet. It is possible that it came from the feral cat that sometimes makes his way to our backyard or wild rabbits or squirrels. It seems that Sandy who had a habit of licking her paws due to her allergies also picked up the larvae, which later turns into worms, once ingested.

In humans eating the raw or undercooked meat of beef, fish, or pork from infected animals is usually the cause of the contamination, as well as from poorly washed produce, unwashed hands of food handlers or contaminated water. It is not surprising that children are most often the unwitting victims of worms. They play in the park along with their dogs and other peoples pets who might be infested with fleas, or the fleas from squirrels, feral cats or rodents, and come in direct contact with the larvae these infected fleas leave behind, while they touch their face and mouths and before you know it they also become carriers of worms.

This brings me to a slight detour, so please buckle up and enjoy the ride while I continue to rant and rave. One of my very worst pet peeves is the body modification of animals. It is just another form of unnecessary mutilation, cruel and barbaric.

Nothing riles me up more than to see animals with their ears clipped, tails docked, de-vocalized, de-clawed, de-beaked etc. It is just plain wrong especially since they never have a choice in the matter and it is rarely the result of medical need.

Although we live in a plastic surgery obsessed society and body modification, which includes extreme plastic surgeries, tattoos, body piercing, etc. is big with humans and being done at an alarming rate, especially among young people, I am not judging those who do, only judging the ones that mutilate their own pets for their personal convenience.

Personally I don't think I would have plastic surgery for cosmetic reasons since I am not that vain, at least not yet, since I believe that aging gracefully is a privilege and not a curse, but I don't see anything wrong with minor surgery, if it genuinely gives a person more self confidence and improves their self image and quality of their lives and they are doing this for themselves and not to please others.

We all know what our best assets are, and at the risk of sounding immodest, I have always been told that I have beautiful hair. It is lush, healthy and glossy. And when people ask me if it is all really mine, since these days most women who seem to have great hair only have fake extensions or implants, I am very fond of saying, "it's the real thing baby!" People pay thousands of dollars on their appearance, and hair is most definitely a precious commodity and I know I am very fortunate in that regard. In the olden days, had I been scalped, my head of hair would have garnered top dollar. However, animals with luxurious fur deserve to keep the skin on their backs and not on somebody else's. Hunting or killing an animal solely for its fur, especially since they are skinned alive, or for sport is beyond inhumane, barbaric and cruel. It is bad enough that some are also killed for food.

We no longer live in pre-historic times where cavemen dressed in animal furs to keep warm. There are so many faux fur options these days, especially for those who like the look and feel of fur. Some women have closets full of real furs that they have not worn in years. Especially now days when it is considered politically incorrect to wear fur, by donating them to wildlife organizations they can greatly help orphaned animals such as bear cubs, lions or seals among others, that have lost their mothers to poachers. It gives the cubs a sense of security and comfort while they sleep and helps to rehabilitate them.

A subject that has always troubled me and been extremely uncomfortable is the killing of animals for food. We are all predators of some sort and we unfortunately often consume another species in order to survive, just as other species consume other species to survive. It has always literally been the survival of the fittest. Although I have not eaten beef, pork, or lamb or anything considered meat for over twenty years, and have not eaten chicken or turkey or anything considered poultry since I was a child, as I once witnessed a chicken being killed for food and it was such a traumatic experience, I am guilty of eating fish. I consider myself to be semi-vegetarian and I truly admire those that have fully committed to be vegan.

I stopped wearing leather clothes since it's explosion in the late 80's, but am guilty of still wearing leather shoes and purses and belts. Over the past years though, I have made the commitment not to purchase any more leather accessories and as the ones that I have are worn down, they are now replaced with fabric or other man-made materials.

Recently, here in California, there is a buzz over the very controversial subject of "foie gras", which translates into "fatty liver" in French. It is the result of force-feeding or "gavage", of a duck or goose enormous amounts of food, mainly corn and fat, with a 15-inch metal pipe that is rammed into their throat to the esophagus several times a day, until its liver becomes abnormally enlarged 12 times over, before it is consumed. Foie gras is considered a delicacy and its origins can be traced back to ancient Egypt, mainly as a food of royalty. It was later popularized throughout Europe and mainly by the French in the 1700's, and is now the world's largest producer and consumer of foie gras, followed by Hungary, Bulgaria and the United

States. In the United Stated there are only two foie gras factories, one in Sonoma California and the other in the Hudson Valley in New York.

The practice of gavage is beyond cruel, extremely inhumane and yet another form of animal abuse, as the tortured animals are held down, often sometimes vomiting and choking on the food that they are forced to swallow. So many animals die during this process that the small percentage that do survive, has made foie gras one of the most expensive foods in the world. The birds are also confined in such small spaces, crammed into filthy feces-ridden wire cages, that they cannot even flap their wings or sit down or turn around during their entire lives. Sometimes their organs rupture from overfeeding, the spleen and kidneys are damaged and they develop tumors in the esophagus. In addition they also develop severe foot infections and gangrene from cuts while standing on wire cages, until they die a slow and painful death.

Unfortunately it has taken thousands of years to ban this barbaric practice. Norway was the first country to ban the production and consumption in the mid 1970's, followed by at least a dozen other countries, and now finally in California after years of pressure from animal activists. The impending law has chefs up in arms, claiming that it will take away their creative freedom, and that no one has the right to tell them what to feed their customers. Consumers and lovers of "food of despair" feel the same way, acting as if they themselves are the victims whose rights are being violated. What about the freedom that was denied those helpless birds held in captivity, against their will, since their very existence? Is it really necessary to also mistreat them before they are consumed for food?

Until I myself became an advocate and activist of humane treatment of all animals and especially the ones who are raised for food, I was unaware, shocked, and horrified at the atrocities conducted in the factory farms of chickens, pigs, cows, sheep to name a few and how unnecessarily and grossly mistreated all the animals are.

All I can say is am glad I never ate foie gras.

I also no longer buy products such as cosmetics that are tested on unsuspecting animals without a voice. Products for humans should only be tested on humans. Lab animals suffer greatly when they are used for experimentation and often end up with horrendous side effects that cause them to have tumors and eventually a slow painful death. To me it's the same as being placed in a concentration camp. In high school I flat out refused to dissect a frog in my physiology class. My teacher understood and admired and respected my point of view, but told me that he would have to lower my grade. I still managed to get a B and it was well worth it.

One thing that drives me completely crazy is seeing people walking or running their dogs in 100-degree weather in full sun, on scorching hot asphalt or cement or even on dry sand as well as brick, paving stones and hot metal surfaces. These compulsive-obsessive, exercise driven people, feel the need to drag their poor animals along for the ride. I see it all the time. The poor animals are panting out of control, on the verge of having heatstroke, and their insensitive owners are completely oblivious to the damage they are causing their supposedly beloved pets, just because they feel comfortable with their cushy shoes. These ignorant people somehow believe their dogs have tough footpads that can withstand any surface and temperature whether scorching or even freezing.

Every year veterinarians see an increase in footpad injuries in the summer, ranging from very serious burns, blisters, limping, bleeding and infection and in the winter, frostbite. After all in nature animals were made to walk only on natural surfaces like grass or dirt and not manmade. During summer months, for the safety of the pet, they should only be walked early in the morning or very late at night when the surfaces have cooled down. It is important to test the surface of the ground with the palm of the hand. A general rule of thumb is if it is too hot for us, it is too hot for the dog.

Recently I came across a situation that really disturbed me. I was driving on the Ventura Freeway around the Calabasas area and spotted what appeared to be a very large toy, a stuffed animal on the side of the road. At first I felt sorry for the kid who lost it's toy, but as I came closer I realized it was real and resembled a cheetah. I found it very odd that it was wearing a pink harness, so I assumed it had been domesticated, which was even odder and it left me feeling very unsettled. I immediately called 911 and they transferred me to Animal Control, who said they would be there right away. I followed up the next day and the officer knew exactly what I was referring to and told me that it was an ocelot, not a cheetah although they look alike, and that unfortunately some people had permits to own them, but most are obtained through the illegal exotic animal trade. The poor animal was dead. Owning a wild animal or certain types of exotic animals never make good household pets, and ultimately more often than not ends up in unnecessary tragedy, as they are not happy living outside their habitat and in captivity.

Wild animals belong in the wild, period.

Another thing that I am completely against is the use of wild animals such as bears, lions, elephants and others in circuses for the ridiculous purpose of entertaining us. These animals are treated with a great deal of cruelty in an effort to "train" them. They deserve to be left alone, just to be, and to be admired from far away. I am also against bullfighting, horse racing, and greyhound racing and countless other methods of coercing animals into doing things that are completely unnatural.

What about those crazy people that believe in balancing the eco system by the aerial shooting of wolfs or bears or other wild animals in their own habitat? Hasn't nature been taking care of itself for thousands of years without our help? Haven't we interfered long enough and practically decimated our planet?

Then there are those people who leave their children and pets in hot, parked cars!!! Over and over again, we hear of babies and animals being left alone with just a slight crack open for ventilation. Temperatures inside parked cars, even on cool days can reach up to 100 degrees and above. In most cases causing heatstroke, brain damage, and even death. Dogs are most often the victims especially because they don't have the ability to sweat and cool themselves off.

There is a new ad campaign in California designed to help animals. It is quite graphic but it gets the message across. It is a photo of a dog inside an oven with the message "Hot Oven . . . Hot Car. It's the same thing." Fortunately it is now a California state law to charge a pet owner with misdemeanor animal endangerment, for which they can face up to six months in jail and if the animal should die as a result, the owner can be charged with felony animal cruelty. Hopefully this law can eventually be in effect nationwide and ideally worldwide someday.

One day while going out to lunch in one of the studios where I worked as a costumer, I came across a situation that was very, very alarming. I found a large black dog that had been left in a scorching hot car for five hours and if I had not noticed him, it would have been eight hours and the dog would have died. The poor dog's water had dried up and he was so weak that he didn't even bark when I got near the window, which was all steamed up, and I am surprised that he was not comatose. I quickly ran inside and asked whose car it was and people were very guarded about telling me since he was the son of a" very famous and important film director" and I was told not to make waves. I kept on asking different people until I finally got a hold of his boss, who was the set decorator, and asked to have the dog owner call me regarding his dog and if it would be alright for me to call the auto club to open the door and let him out. When I spoke to the dog owner, he told me that he had not intended to be gone that long and got busy with other things and lost track of time, but that he felt his dog would be fine because he had left him in the shade in the morning.

Well guess what? Shade moves! Dogs can still die in the shade. It's the heat that kills!

With the help of the auto club, who did not charge us for coming out, and a couple of other guys, we pried the high security expensive foreign SUV door open and set the poor dog free. I cleaned up his water bowl and filled it with clean fresh cool water, which he slurped as he trembled, and later relieved himself by the huge shady tree nearby. The look of gratitude on the distressed dog's face broke my heart.

The "director's son" finally showed up right before closing time and thanked me for saving his dog's life. I told him that if he really loved his dog he should leave him at home where he would be much happier and safer, or to take him to one of the many pet daycare centers that are popping up all over town and which he could very well afford. If I had known then what I know now, I would not have wasted any time. I would have just called 911 and have him slapped with a misdemeanor.

If it were possible to catch and fine every person in this country who has ever left a child or pet inside a boiling hot car even for five minutes, that alone could very well help to solve the national deficit problem.

Retractable leashes, very dangerous! Most people don't know how to use them properly and they are sometimes as good as having no leash at all. With lengths usually ranging from 15 feet to 25 feet, it is very hard to control a pet that is so far away from their owner, that they are vulnerable to getting attacked by other animals or being run over by a car.

There was an incident at a well known pet supply store where a dog was allowed to wander three aisles over with the retractable leash on and he ran face to face with an aggressive dog (why was a dangerous animal brought inside the store?) who was not in the mood to play, viciously attacked him, and the poor dog later died from the fatal wounds.

Oftentimes the person handling the retractable leash also gets injured from getting it tangled at a high speed or because they were not quick enough to react and reel their pets in to safety. Retractable leashes are responsible for a surprising number of injuries each year according to statistics collected by the Consumer Product Safety Commission. The most common cases reported were burns and cuts to the skin, when the nylon cord/tape/belt gets wrapped around the owner, dog, or a bystander nearby. The more serious injuries involve the eyes, face and neck as well as broken bones and amputation of fingers and sometimes limbs and accidental death. Although most have a warning label, these leashes are now being banned in some places and never used by the majority of dog trainers. After all the whole purpose of using any kind of leash is to keep our pets safe and out of harm's way.

Parents who get puppies or kittens, bunnies or baby chicks to name a few species, for their tots as if they were living toys! As with anything else, very young children lose interest and tire of them quickly, and are not capable of caring for the pet in any capacity.

Unless parents themselves are prepared to raise the baby pets along with their own children, which is hard enough, and make a full time commitment they should think twice beforehand. Sadly many of these animals will end up in shelters when parents realize they can't mange their own children much less a puppy or kitten or other pet.

People who feed other peoples pets without their owner's permission? It's not okay. Some animals have medical conditions that require a special diet and even a small piece of the wrong food could have drastic consequences. Also, the well-meaning person might not be aware of which foods are toxic even to healthy pets.

Above all, I am deeply disturbed by the increase of abuse and violent, despicable, repulsive, and perverse crimes against all kinds of animals, especially by children. Where are their parents? Or does it come as a result of neglectful or abusive parents? Some of these children may have witnessed abuse of some sort or have themselves been victims of such, and controlling and overpowering and inflicting pain in helpless innocent creatures gives them a distorted and false sense of empowerment. This gives them license to move on to humiliating and abusing people in one form or another. The majority of serial killers that we read about, start out by taunting, bullying, tormenting, torturing and brutalizing and killing animals at a very young age. Once they are able to get away with it and thrill of the kill of smaller things is gone, they move on to people their own age and eventually to grownups and once the high that they get from killing one person fails to satisfy, they become serial and ultimately mass murderers. They are impervious to pain and suffering by others.

Although I don't claim to be an expert on this subject or any other, it is constantly in the news and the story is pretty much always the same. More and more children today seem to be missing a sensitivity chip as well as compassion and empathy and appear to be genuinely emotionally detached and mean spirited. I recently drove by an elementary school and noticed a big sign posted on the fence that said "NO GUNS ALLOWED ON CAMPUS." Has technology created a monster??? Have we raised a society of robotic young people lacking in social skills and incapable of communicating on a personal level because they are so used to pushing buttons for instant gratification? This brings me to another question. Are we all born innocent or are some people born essentially a bad seed? Or is it a learned behavior?

Another very alarming epidemic on the rise these days is domestic abuse against family pets. The animals fall prey to misdirected anger by the same people that abuse their spouses, partners, parents and children. Most often it is women and children or the elderly that are the victims. They are afraid to leave because they have been threatened to be killed and to have the only thing that they value in their lives, their source of comfort, and that is their beloved pets, harmed or killed as well. It is a never-ending vicious cycle that we hear about more and more today.

Are people angrier today? Or is it the fact that their rage is getting more publicity as some very brave people have come forward to share their painful stories and let others know that they are not alone, and that there are ways to seek help in a safe manner.

Fortunately due to raised awareness, there are now more anti-cruelty task forces to protect animals, as well as animal forensics, that enable to prosecute the abusers sending a message out there to those perpetrators that there are severe consequences to face and pay for their cruelty. People that close their eyes and keep silent to such horrific matters and are passive bystanders, in essence condone that behavior because they did nothing to prevent or stop it. The only way to end cruelty is through humane education, which should be mandatory in all schools from kindergarten to high school, and to take an active role in the various forms of activism either by donating, volunteering or by helping to change laws regarding animal welfare. Also I believe that by teaching children to be kind to animals they will develop self-esteem and learn to respect and be patient and kind to others.

Currently in the United States alone there are approximately 4 million perfectly beautiful, innocent and healthy homeless dogs and cats killed each year by what the animal shelters call "euthanization", simply because there is no budget or room to house them. I call it cold-blooded murder! Surprisingly some shelter workers make more money than the average schoolteacher and some have even been found to be guilty of committing atrocities against the very animals they are paid to protect. That is why I believe there should be hidden surveillance cameras for those working in animal shelters, to protect the animals from human predators who might have ulterior motives and sadistic tendencies and get a perverse pleasure out of harming unsuspecting victims.

There is so much abuse going on in this world, especially to the forgotten elderly in nursing homes, to women in third world countries where they have no rights and to innocent children who are victims of sexual predators and child labor, just to mention a few examples.

But for all the bad things happening on our planet there are also some positive changes. I admire famous people who use their celebrity to raise awareness to certain causes. An example of that would be George Clooney who has put Darfur on the map to so many people who did not know about the genocide there. Matt Damon has helped bring fresh drinking water to those who cannot avail themselves of those resources. Having clean, fresh water not only for drinking but also for bathing and sanitation in general, should not be a privilege but a human right. We take so much for granted in the United States. Although there are so many others who are lending a helping hand, the ones I mentioned above are very diverse in nature and equally important. My list of issues goes on and on, but I devoted this chapter mainly as a way to help animals and these are just a few of the many concerns that I have.

Chapter Fourteen

THE BIG MOVE

Fred and I had been planning to rebuild his parent's house for some time and my brother Randy, who is an architect, had done a beautiful design of our dream home. The plans were almost complete, when we decided that it was probably best to sell the house since Sandy was having a very hard time climbing up the flight of steps and going outside had become an impossible ordeal that gave us all a great deal of anxiety.

The time frame several builders had given us was approximately one year or more and we couldn't wait that long. It became a daily struggle getting Sandy back up to our living room after her walks, and it was heartbreaking watching her make several attempts on her own to climb all those stairs before she would start whimpering out of frustration. It was even harder for me to try to carry Sandy up the flight of steps without her becoming more agitated and trying to bite me, and also the fact that she was too heavy for me. Carrying Sandy has always been like wrangling a small alligator. She is a proud and fierce little sheepdog and I better not forget it! All these years I've had to put on my winter jacket and gloves to avoid any problems even in one hundred degree weather.

We narrowed down the search for our home and our number one requirement was that it be one story and have a good size backyard for Sandy. We went to open houses every weekend and started doing virtual tours on the Internet, and that is how we found our home. It was the one that most closely resembled our dream home even though it is a lot smaller but ironically it had also been designed and completely remodeled by an architect. We also love the neighborhood; it is quiet and peaceful with lots of trees.

Although we are very disappointed that we didn't build our dream home, we are hoping that Randy builds it for himself one day.

A few days before moving, I took Sandy to the new house so that she would start to become familiar with it and had already brought some of her toys, blankets, and water bowl beforehand, as well as some of our belongings. Instead, when she entered the house she was bewildered. Sandy already knew something was brewing as we had been packing our things and she had become increasingly agitated.

The night before the actual move we slept at my mom's house where Sandy would spend the next day while we were dealing with the movers, because seeing them taking our furniture away would be very traumatic for her, since she had already dealt with that during Barton's death, aside from the fact that she won't allow strangers in our home. Sandy is the best guard dog in the entire world and an even better security system than most.

We picked Sandy up before dark and took her back to her new home. After all we bought the home just for her, it was the only decent thing to do. As soon as Sandy came inside, she started frantically sniffing everything, going from room to room and looking at us with a puzzled look in her eyes. Sandy was very anxious and nervous and was pacing back and forth until she wore herself out.

When we went to sleep that first night, all together in the same room at last, Sandy went over to Fred's side of the bed.

I said, "No Sandy, that is the wrong side, Mommy sleeps here". "Come here little girl, this side", I said demonstrating. "Sandy come here", I said patting her pet bed next to my side. But Sandy wasn't budging.

I told Fred that she was probably confused with all the commotion, but I could not wipe the smirk from his face, which later turned to a full-blown belly laugh, as I kept on making excuses for Sandy.

I seriously don't think I have ever heard Fred laugh that hard, except for a time early in our marriage, when Fred was watching a TV documentary on baseball. I had asked him who Hans Wagoner was and Fred answered, "He is one of the all time greats in baseball history." "As a matter of fact they used to call him "the flying Dutchman." An hour later, still watching the same program, he said, "You see that guy?" "His name is Ty Cobb, he is one of the all time greats in baseball history." I was so confused because he had repeated almost the same thing that I said "How come the Dutchman changed his name to Ty Cobb?" I had somehow managed to make a tossed salad out of all the information Fred had given me, and Fred in disbelief could not stop laughing.

Sandy had a lot of explaining to do the next morning, so I gave my little girl five minutes to get her story straight, but she wasn't barking.

I sat on the kitchen floor next to her and looked her straight in the eye, nose to nose, but she just looked away as she always does when she doesn't want to deal with things.

"Why did you do it?" I said, "What was the reason?" "How could you betray your Mommy that loves you?"

Sandy then put her paw on my knee, and looked at me with those eyes, those irresistible eyes, knowing that she has the ability to make me melt. I am fond of saying to her "where did those little eyes come from?" But all wasn't forgiven that easily.

"Mommy sacrificed for you, Mommy slept on the carpet for you, Mommy home cooks all your meals and makes all your biscuits, Mommy has a mobile groomer give you a coiffure, manicure and pedicure, Mommy doesn't do that for herself," and on and on . . .

I could not believe that little Benedict Arnold!

The next night Sandy did the same thing, so I tried to bribe the Sheltie with a biscuit leading her over to my side of the bed. She followed me, took the bait and ate the treat, and then returned to Fred's side. By now Fred was laughing hysterically and worse, he was gloating. He was very amused by it all and said "Let's face it, Sandy loves me more", trying to further irritate me.

I explained that Sandy was just trying to make up for lost time. And that is exactly what she has done ever since. She will start out sleeping on Fred's side and will migrate to my side of the bed in the middle of the night and onto her bed, next to me.

I finally got even when Fred could not get out of bed, because Sandy was all sprawled out over on his side, and he was afraid of stepping on her, so he had to climb out of bed through the front. Not an easy thing for a big guy to do. I then told him about the old Chinese proverb "He who laughs last, laughs better." Actually I made that up.

Once we settled in our new home we had to deal with the gardeners and the pool man. I had a picket fence installed to protect Sandy from the swimming pool, since not all dogs know how to swim or exit a pool, and I wasn't taking any chances. Tragically so many pets drown unnecessarily when simple precautions are available. Sandy is an indoor dog and I never leave her unattended in the garden. I am always concerned about pets that are left outdoors unprotected from the elements and especially by predators. I cannot completely trust that the gardeners or pool man will keep the outside gates closed at all times, and risk having her run out, or have a stray dog, or other animal run into our property and attack her.

As a matter of fact I wrote an article that was published for **The Pet Press** and I will re-print it in an effort to save lives.

Pets and Pool Safety

By Sandy Spiwak-Wallin

Although I do not claim to be an expert on animals by any means, I do know one thing, not all dogs know how to swim. And the ones that do don't necessarily know how to exit a swimming pool. Especially dogs who unexpectedly end up in a pool while chasing after something at great speed. They panic and eventually drown.

An animal's perception of depth is very different than ours. Sadly, drowning accidents can be easily avoided by taking certain precautions such as enclosing a pool with a fence, pool cover or using a pool ramp, (which dogs have to be taught how to use), or a baby gate on the back door leading to the pool. Another popular choice these days is to use a life jacket available at pet stores and in catalogues. Better yet, simply keep pets indoors or temporarily confined in a safe area until one is able to keep an eye on them at all times, just like children.

How many times have we heard, "I just let the dog out for one second?" It is precisely in that split second when most tragedies occur.

It was in that split second that my two-year-old niece almost drowned while chasing after her cat that went into the pool, while her caretaker momentarily looked away. And it was in that split second that my friend's dog died last week.

After a short swim my friend, who "always" keeps the pool cover on, went inside for "just one moment" while the dog was outside. When she returned, to her horror, disbelief and shock, her dog had drowned. She tried in vain to revive him, leaving her completely devastated and feeling very guilty.

This is the third time over the years that someone that I know, has lost a dog to drowning.

When we moved into a house that had a pool, the first thing that I did was to put up a very sturdy vinyl picket fence double the height of my dog, across the yard blocking off the swimming pool. No, we don't have children, but I was not taking any chances.

After much criticism from many people for spending "that kind of money for a dog", (if they only knew what I really spend) and for being so overprotective and paranoid, I would rather be safe than sorry.

Living in times when gardeners, pool men, maids, babysitters, caretakers, workmen etc. enter our homes and gardens on a constant basis, and at inconsistent hours and sometimes on unexpected days, it is good to be prepared. We can avoid heartbreak by instructing and constantly reminding everybody, especially children and elderly people, to keep the gates and doors closed. That way we can prevent our beloved pets from running away, having unfortunate accidents, and possibly drowning.

*   *   *

A few months after writing this article however, I had overheard from the local veterinarian's office about a large dog that had just drowned while a family friend was babysitting. The woman in charge could not find the dog anywhere and thought he had jumped over the fence and ran away when in fact he had slipped under the pool cover that was not strong enough to support his weight therefore trapping him. The pool man discovered his dead body a few days later.

The one thing I allow Sandy to do, with my supervision, is to herd the gardeners in only when they are behind the picket fence, pruning the flowers, and no machinery is being used. They in turn graciously indulge my beloved little sheepdog. As far as the pool man is concerned, Sandy can't stand him. Every week she waits for him by the door to the backyard in a predatory mode, on the exact day and time so she can bark at him. I always have him call me beforehand so that I can keep Sandy inside. I don't want her getting too agitated.

I thought that once we had moved into our new home Sandy's delinquent ways would be behind her, but that was not to be the case. I could not understand why Sandy kept on going in and out of my bathroom, and caught her inside my shower several times. What was the fascination all of a sudden? Then one night while I was brushing my teeth with the door slightly ajar, she pushed it wide open with her nose and got inside the shower stall and quickly ran away with something in her mouth. I chased after her all over the house with toothpaste dripping from my mouth, and realized she had taken a bar of soap that had fallen to the bottom, and proceeded to eat it, just as she had done with the ballpoint pen awhile back. The more I yelled at her to stop, the faster she chewed it. Sandy was in "mine mode", possessive and aggressive. I ran to the front door and rang the doorbell hoping that she would start barking, and in the process drop it but that did not happen in this instance, because Sandy was no longer buying "the old ring-the-doorbell trick", and Fred and I were freaking out.

The Sheltie can be a tough negotiator in situations like this, but I was fully prepared to up the ante. I ran to the kitchen and got a piece of deli fresh roasted turkey, which we normally have as a special reward treat, and threw it in the far opposite direction, so as she ran to get it, it would force her to drop the soap, but Sandy's challenge at the moment was to figure out how to keep the bar of soap in her mouth while getting to eat the turkey at the same time. I think that is called gluttony. When Sandy finally realized it was not going to work out she reluctantly gave in and dropped part of the left over soap she had not yet ingested, while giving me just enough time to quickly pick it up, before she would run back to reclaim it. It is never easy to stay a step ahead of the little sheepdog, because Sandy always has an agenda, and is highly unpredictable.

I wrapped up the left over piece of soap and we took her to the pet emergency clinic where we waited for several hours. I could not believe how busy the place was, especially late at night. Patients were seen not on a first come basis, but rather on the level of urgency. Everybody had a story to tell, and I realized there are a lot of very mischievous pets out there, which can do no wrong like ours. A Jack Russell Terrier was seen first because he had jumped up onto a table and ate an entire box of chocolates, which could be fatal. Bar soap was not considered as dangerous.

The vet finally gave Sandy an amorphine injection to induce vomiting, but it took awhile. Luckily Sandy's belly was still full from her dinner, so she had a cushion, which made it a little easier to reject the soap pieces. The doctor gave me a liquid antibiotic to take home where she continued to purge through the night into next morning until all the pieces of soap were gone.

Apparently Sandy shares my appreciation for delicately scented, European triple-milled soaps, one of the small luxuries in life. We now keep all the bathroom doors closed.

I said it before and I will say it again, "all dogs are opportunists."

Our new home has enabled Sandy's self-confidence to soar. These days Sandy is getting more and more in touch with her inner sheepdog and her home is her castle. She loves to run outside into our backyard to bark at anything and everything. She especially loves to shoo away the two crows that have taken residence in our yard. They fly in daily and strut across our backyard with such attitude that I have given them both names. Alfred Hitchcock and Edgar Allen Poe. If I may say so, the Goth-like boys are very dapper.

Sandy's new world also includes squirrels, three little lizards that we named Lizzie, Izzie, and Izz, in order of size. Izz being the smallest is a total of two inches from nose to tail. She is very shy and is always hiding from me when I spot her sunbathing at her usual hangouts. Also there is a wide array of butterflies that completely fascinate Sandy and birds, including our very own Woody Woodpecker with the red spiky punk hairdo.

The newest addition to our wildlife family, which we automatically inherited when we bought the house, is a darling little brown wild bunny with white ears and a cottontail and he lives inside our red geranium bushes near the white picket fence. He is always startled and hops out when the sprinklers go on, which is how I discovered him to begin with. Occasionally two ducks in particular, a pair, one a mallard and the other a spotted brown and white female, have flown in several times during spring time over the past years, and have frolicked and swam in our pool, had lunch and later sunbathed before flying away. I am always sad to see them go.

Then of course there are the next-door cats, which occasionally make their way into our backyard. The black and white one, a female, is very sweet and shy and mainly walks on the block fence dividing our homes, but Smoke, the name I gave to the charcoal grey male cat because he is so elusive and mysterious, is also much more mischievous. When Sandy chases him away, he always has this indignant look on his face as if saying, "what did I do?"

More than anything, Sandy loves to bark at and chase "Rocky" away. She could be fast asleep and the next second flip over, run and hysterically bark by the back door for us to let her out, because she smells a squirrel.

Every time we said, "where's the squirrel?" Sandy would go crazy and charge towards the door. So one day in order not to agitate her, I avoided the word "squirrel", and when Fred asked me why I had not yet let Sandy out, I said because "Rocky" was outside. Rocky is the iconic squirrel from the "Rocky and Bullwinkle" cartoon. Apparently Sandy knew who "Rocky" was! Maybe Barton had told her about him, because as soon as I said it, she went ballistic and does so every time we say "Rocky."

We occasionally run into Jake, the handsome Golden Retriever next door, when we go for our daily walks around the block. He is a big oversized pup, and because our neighbor knows about Sandy's background, and how fearful she is of other dogs he keeps him at a distance, but it is obvious that Jake has a total crush on Sandy. Whenever he sees her, he wags and wags his tail, and tries to get closer, and stares at her with adoring eyes. But Sandy completely ignores him, the same way she did with the Lhasa Apso brothers, Buddy and Stuart, who lived in our former townhouse. My little girl is such a heartthrob and a heartbreaker.

My favorite moments with Sandy are when she sits outside in the backyard patio overlooking the garden and pool, while I am sitting at the kitchen table with the door wide open and I can see her pointing her nose up towards the sky as high up as it will go, taking it all in, smelling all the smells, seeing all the sights, hearing all the sounds, and contemplating nature. Those moments as well as the times when Sandy comes and quietly sits by my side when I am watching TV can only be described as serene and blissful.

Sandy is an observer much like me. I used the be the kind of child that would miss the school bus because I was busy appreciating the beautiful bougainvillea at the bus stop, or patiently watching for an ant to go from point A to B with a bread crumb on it's back, or waiting for caterpillars to turn into butterflies in my special science class jar. I was independent and never needed to be entertained, because I was hardly ever bored, since I found so many things in life interesting.

Our house in Guatemala, which can be described as mid-century modern, timeless, open and airy and light filled, truly an original architectural structure, had two flights of floor to ceiling glass windows overlooking one of several garden atriums, and I could easily spend hours being mesmerized by the curtain-like patterns the rain would leave behind. It is not surprising that our house inspired my brother Randy to become an architect.

The visual stimulation that I experienced in this most picturesque country with its explosion of colorful flowers, volcanoes, mountains, rivers, lakes, and villages and its native people dressed in intricate multicolor hand-woven textiles, each native of Mayan descent had a different costume representing their village, had a direct impact on me seeking careers in the world of fashion, costume and the arts.

It is amazing how two people growing up in the same household can be so different in their style. Randy's artistic work has a great deal of finesse and sophistication while mine is a little bolder, more colorful and playful.

I have always been a dreamer and observer but not much of a participator. I always liked doing my own thing, leading some people to think of me as having been somewhat detached especially in my younger days, although I was always very friendly and social. When Sandy came into my life, she brought me down to a different kind of reality, teaching me about priorities and not wasting time, and gave me the wings and voice that I didn't know that I had. Because of Sandy I developed a certain type of self-confidence and openness that was missing before.

We have been living at the new home for almost four years now, and life seems to keep on getting more unpredictable as time goes by. I have basically always been in good health, so when I started to experience numbness and tingling in my left arm all the way down to my fingertips, I basically ignored it. After all I had just had a complete physical a few months before and been given a clean bill of health. Thinking it was nothing serious, as it kept on coming and going over a period of time. I though the pain that I was feeling was due to a sprain, or that I slept on it too long, or maybe even be carpal tunnel syndrome. But as the pain became more intense to excruciating, I finally went to see a doctor when the symptoms would not disappear.

As Dr. Garb felt my pulse and blood pressure, he discovered there was none on my left arm and asked the nurse to bring him a stethoscope that works. She informed him that it did, but gave him another one anyway. He then shook his head and frowned and looked up without trying to alarm me and asked me to wait in the waiting room. In the meantime he was making pre-op arrangements with a vascular surgeon for me to have an angiogram.

When I met Dr. Rafidi, one of the foremost vascular surgeons in the world, he informed me that my life was in serious danger, as well as the possibility of losing my arm, and that the surgery that I was about to have was very delicate and of epic proportions. The sudden information was too much to process, so I did not even have time to get scared, because I was still in shock and disbelief over what was happening to me. I went to see him on Friday and he would be operating on Monday morning.

But my biggest worry was Sandy. The night before my surgery I sent Fred a two-page e-mail with very detailed instructions for Sandy's care. Even though he often fed her and let her out, Sandy had certain vitamins and other supplements that she took at different times and with different meals. It provided Fred with a brief moment of comic relief in the midst of all the worry, because not even premature newborn babies in ICU get that many instructions.

The morning of my surgery I had my cousin Sorel, who is one of the most dependable and punctual people that I have ever known, and an early bird unlike me, pick me up because I needed Fred to stay home to feed and take Sandy out. He would later be meeting us as the hospital with my mom and brother. Sandy was in a deep slumber as I was leaving and I decided to sneak out as to not wake her up because it was still very early, dark and very cold. In hindsight that was a big mistake, because when Sandy woke up I was nowhere to be found, and she did not see me for eleven days. She was confused and did not know what happened to me, especially because she always sees me leave and then return.

After performing an angiogram where dye is injected into the bloodstream to see where the blockage is, Dr. Rafidi discovered that I had a subclavian aneurysm near the collarbone, as well as three blood clots on my left arm. He performed the second delicate surgery the following day. Basically I had back-to-back anesthesia. He said that in all the years he has been practicing medicine, that he had never seen a case like mine, that it was extremely rare, especially because I did not fit the profile, and that they would be discussing it at medical conferences and writing about in medical journals. I truly hope that other people may benefit from my pain in the future so that it all will not have been in vain.

I was in the ICU for three days, and I must say that it is the noisiest place in the entire world. I was hooked up to all these wires, oxygen, and IV's that kept on beeping forever, and nurses kept on waking me up to take my vital signs. Around five in the morning the second shift of doctors and nurses would start to come in and the noise emanating from the hallway was reminiscent of a high school corridor. Not being a morning person myself, I've never understood how people can be so cheerful so early in the morning. It is almost obscene as far as I am concerned. Then there was the lovely swirling floor-cleaning machine, which smelled of lemon and ammonia. That smell alone could kill you. The whole experience was very surrealistic.

When I was a little bit more alert after some of the anesthesia had worn off, I was afraid to look over at my left arm because I did not know what to expect. In an emotionally detached way I slowly peeked over and was incredibly grateful to still have my arm and did not mind that I had an incision from my inner elbow all the way down to my wrist. I also had two very large incisions on my neck and clavicle where they found the aneurysm.

A couple of days later, my brother went to pick up some of my belongings to take back to the hospital where I would be staying for eight days, and noticed that Sandy was very depressed and nonresponsive. Normally she does not let anyone inside the house without making a big scandal, but Sandy didn't care and was very distant barely looking up. My neighbor

John periodically came over to help Fred, who had a broken shoulder at the time, to open up canned goods or jars because he could not lift certain things. He also reported the same thing; that Sandy was not the same.

As soon as I got out of ICU, I had Fred put Sandy on the phone just so she could hear my voice. I kept telling her how she was a good girl and that mommy loves and misses her, and that mommy was coming home soon. Fred reported that she perked her ears and then I could hear her bark. That made me smile.

Because the hospital was filled to capacity, once I was out of ICU I was transferred to a room with another woman, the patient from hell. She complained all day and night about her kidney stones, argued with doctors and nurses and never slept. She had the light on all night long not allowing me to get some rest, while she watched TV at full volume and played with video games in her laptop computer, being totally inconsiderate. At first I felt kind of bad for her because I know first hand from Fred's experience, that kidney stones can be extremely painful, but all my sympathy flew out the window when she ordered a corned beef sandwich with "extra pickles" from the nearby deli. Nobody could stand her and she was sent home two days later, because she had eaten when she was not supposed to, and the doctors had to reschedule her surgery. I was thrilled.

Then came my next roommate whom the nurses referred to as "Mama", and she was the quintessential drama queen. She cried, "Just let me die, I don't want to be a burden on my children." "I just want to be in my home with my pills and my TV." But actually she was a very sweet older and endearing lady with a lot of issues, one of them being afraid of the dark. At this point I was delirious from lack of sleep and pain and begged the nurses to please turn off the light, but they thought I would have better luck convincing "Mama" with that. Softly I said to her "Don't be afraid, I am right here next to you, go to sleep" and quoting directly from the movie "Babe", and feigning an English accent pretending to be the gentle and maternal cattle dog I said, "Don't worry my dear, I'll take care you." I don't know if it was the authority in my voice or the desperation, but Mama fell asleep in an instant, allowing me to finally turn off the lights.

My mind was racing with all kinds of thoughts and when my whole life started to flash before my eyes, I felt this was the beginning of the end for me. I reminisced about my childhood in Guatemala, where I lived from the ages of two to twelve. Remembering when our nannies used to coerce us into turning off the lights and going to bed early, instilling fear in us, so that "La Siguanaba" or "La Llorona", sinister female figures from Guatemalan folklore, would not come to get us and take us away never to return. These haunting tales were distorted; in an effort to tell us that obedient children are not taken away. It always worked. Those nannies had authority and we never challenged them. That is what I call manipulation at it's very finest.

I kept visualizing a field with millions of ladybugs on the school grounds where I used to play during recess. Sometimes I would borrow a few ladybugs and put them inside a glass jar with holes at the top and take them home during lunch, and returned them afterwards to the exact same spot, which I marked with leaves or twigs, because I worried that their parents might be looking for them.

In Guatemala in those days, most schools and businesses closed for two hours much like in the European countries, and people got to see their families during lunch, which was the main meal of the day.

When "Mama" was checking out a few days later while I was walking in the hallway, she apologized for being "such a bad roommate", and I said, "Are you kidding? You were the best roommate I ever had." I never had any roommates in my life before coming to the hospital, and compared to the deli-eating shrew, Mama was a complete angel.

She said "Promise me one thing my dear, because you are so thin and frail, promise me that you are going to eat a lot and get your strength back", and I said "Mama, don't you worry, the next time we meet you are going to see the new and improved version of me." Mama let out a big laugh and gave me an even bigger hug and off she went.

The next day I was sent to a private room until the end of my stay. Thank you, dear God of Mercy for that.

Soon after, the nurse's aides who had taken a liking to me started pampering me and would come to visit often in between their duties so that my family, who rarely left my side and slept in the hospital, could get some rest. My brother Randy, whom I can only describe as the kindest person that I have ever known with a noble quality that is extremely rare, would actually help me brush my teeth. I insisted that he go home to sleep in his comfortable bed, but he would only go home to shower and would alternate with my mom, or Fred, or Sorel and was right back at my side.

It is so important to have a loving and supportive family, especially when the hospital has few nurses who are overwhelmed with their duties, and getting help could take a really long time. It is a known fact that patients without families to overlook their care are often neglected and ignored. I was very fortunate and grateful.

Even the woman in charge of nutrition came to ask me what type of food would be appetizing so that she could prepare it for me because she noticed that I was hardly eating. The lack of food in my system combined with the amount of drugs through the IV and a low-grade fever, made me black out and pass out. It was one of the strangest experiences that I ever had. All I remember is that I became extremely dizzy after a brief walk with the physical therapist, and I sat down and felt everything around me spinning out of control until everything went dark and I slid onto the floor. I heard people screaming around me as I came to, and was put onto a stretcher by several nurses who carried me back onto the bed.

I was later brought a custom made sandwich that was fantastic because it was made with love and I ate the whole thing.

A really nice and beautiful nurse from India came to make the night rounds and asked me if I wanted to eat anything and all of a sudden I had the craving for chocolate ice cream, even though I rarely eat it when I am home. It was already eleven at night so I asked her if the market nearby delivered to the hospital and she said she had a better idea. She had the key to the kitchen and would get me some. She became my "ice cream connection" for the next three late nights. There was an exciting element about that because it was our little secret and this was the closest feeling I ever got to using illicit drugs, aside from the morphine and drug cocktail that I was on, which made up for all the drugs I never took in a lifetime!

We had all decided that it would be best for me to recover post surgery at my mom's house, since Fred would have a hard time taking care of me with a broken shoulder. Besides Fred is not a cook. Although I was very anxious to see Sandy again, my mom convinced me that it would be better for me to settle in at her house a few days before reuniting with Sandy who might jump all over me and force me to lose my balance and hurt me. Both of us would again be staying with her for the next three months. Before checking out of the hospital my mom asked Dr. Rafidi if I was going be all right and recover fully and he said, "Your daughter is going to recover faster than you are."

I will always be extremely grateful to both Dr. Keith Garb and Dr. Fuad Rafidi for acting quickly and saving my life.

Once I was out of the hospital and recovering at my mom's we made arrangements with Luke, Sandy's groomer, to help Fred bring Sandy and her belongings over to my mom's house. There was a great deal of anticipation surrounding our long-at-last reunion. I was lying down on the living room couch waiting for her, expecting Sandy to run over towards me in a sort of frenzy, but instead she seemed disoriented, confused and aloof. It made me very sad.

During the time that I was in the hospital Sandy was very distressed and started to lose her fur in chunks. Her separation anxiety caused her to chew herself all over and she developed a skin infection, which required the use of antibiotics as well as anti-inflammatory medications. Being away from me for that long and being away from her home and usual surroundings and routine, even though Sandy had stayed at my mom's during my other previous surgeries, was adding to her insecurities and nervousness.

As I was making my post surgery adjustments, I decided to stay away from painkillers once I was out of the hospital. I tried to grin and bear it, and thought that I would heal faster that way, without so much medication. As a result I was very restless and could not sleep and tried watching some TV as a way of distracting myself from my discomfort and pain. During that time they were broadcasting a special benefit concert by Barbra Streisand whom I have admired for years, as she is one of the most gifted singers and actors, among other things.

But that's not what I was impressed with. It was actually how much her little doggie, a white fluff-ball, whom the TV crews showed in between her songs, adored her! Wherever you might be out there in the world Barbra, I just want you to know that you are worthy!

With very few choices to watch at 3 am, I discovered the world of infomercials. I could not believe all the beautiful jewelry available in a reverse auction at bargain prices but being the sort of a girl that I am, I can definitely appreciate beautiful things, although I don't necessarily have to own them. Instead, my practical side led me to find a steam mop on another channel much more appealing, so I decided to buy it. I also bought an anti snoring device for Fred and a food dehydrator for Sandy so that it would give her homemade biscuits the right amount of crisp that I could not get from baking them. I can now understand how easily people get hooked on these TV shopping networks. Beforehand I wondered how these people managed to stay in business since they were practically giving the stuff away, until I realized that there is a whole other universe of nocturnal people out there shopping instead of sleeping.

It did not take long for my credit card company to call my home to report some very unusual charges at an even more unusual time of day. Once I confirmed Fred's suspicions, he just laughed.

When we were all together back home again things improved vastly for Sandy and she was on her way to becoming her usual self. Animals are creatures of habit and change of any kind is very upsetting to them.

Last winter I received a phone call with a familiar number and at first I was really excited thinking, "it must be Berta", but it was her son-in-law telling me that she had passed. I knew that she had been ill for a while and had gone to live with her brother, but every now and then we could catch up by phone or by holiday cards and I had invited her to come and stay with us in our new home many times, telling her that I would cook for her and fatten her up, because she had lost a lot of weight, and that we would hang out by the pool reminiscing about old times, but she never made it. Her death was deeply felt by all my family who had come to think of her as an extended family member during the time she had cared for Bernice, Fred's mom, Jack, my late father-in-law, Barton and Sandy "The Sheltie" and myself during my various surgeries.

A year later while Fred and I were both home one afternoon, we heard these blood-curdling screams from Sandy and we both ran to her side. She had been lying down by the fireplace floor, which is marble and very slippery and cold, where she often cools her belly. We don't know exactly what happened, but Sandy could not move her back legs, was struggling to get her grip, was trembling and in shock and tried to crawl onto her pet bed as she kept on screaming. I tried to help her but Sandy would not let me and she would not stop crying and was getting hysterical.

At first I thought that maybe her toenail had gotten caught in her fur as she tried to scratch herself but that was not the case. I gently petted her until I was able to get her to lie on her side and calmed her down until we were able to get help. I am so grateful that she was not alone when this horrible ordeal happened, because the consequences could have been even more drastic.

We called a vet who supposedly made house calls but he was not available, so we called our nearby vet and had him send over David, a vet tech, who has helped us administer Sandy's meds in he past. He put a blanket over Sandy and was able to carry her and laid her on my lap as he drove us back to the clinic. Fred followed us.

Our nearby vet took ex-rays and confirmed that her right hind leg was broken and that she would need surgery right away. She was given an analgesic injection and I brought and fed her dinner and she spent the night at the vet. Sandy was picked up the next morning by another vet that she was referred to, which specializes in orthopedic surgery, and we followed behind. Both vets had never seen a fracture like this and believe that over a period of time her femur bone became weak, had a hairline fracture and just split, shattering and tearing into the muscle. She broke her upper thigh where it joins with the hip, the worst possible place for a fracture. The surgeon was originally going to put a plate on her bone but instead put a pin because the bone was too fractured and not strong enough to support it.

The surgical vet said that the tissue surrounding the bone did not look very good and took a biopsy. In the meantime surgery went well and Sandy was home the day after. The vet personally brought her back to our home because we could not carry her and she had to be handled a certain way after the delicate operation. He ordered Sandy to be confined to a small area and to restrict her movement in order to promote healing. I watched over her 24/7 taking time off from work completely, and slept with her in the guest bedroom where I moved her comfortable big bolster orthopedic bed. Instead of closing the door I put up a baby gate so she could still see out into the other rooms, and especially Fred in our master bedroom.

It was very hard taking care of her overall needs because Sandy was in pain, agitated and in a great deal of discomfort even with the pain killers and could only be lifted with a towel rolled underneath her back legs for support to help her walk. It was especially hard getting Sandy to go outside to the backyard to go potty and she would sometimes hold it for over 12-18 hours, driving us crazy just thinking of her discomfort, yet she refused to use the potty pads I had lined the carpet with in the bedroom.

I often called my lovely neighbor Michelle for her help. Sometimes I would hear her sitting outside in her backyard patio with company, but she would always drop everything and come over even in the middle of the night, helping us to coax Sandy outside. I ordered a special sling from a pet catalog and had them ship it overnight, thinking it was going to help, but Sandy hated it and wouldn't let me use it, becoming aggressive if I even tried.

She also refused to be carried and tried to bite when being handled. My stoic Sandy was determined to walk on her own, just like a toddler taking her first baby steps, falling down soon after. To add insult to injury the majority of the floors in our home, except for the bedrooms and hallway, are wood, travertine, or marble and very slippery. This was especially bad for Sandy because of her post surgery lack of balance.

It breaks our heart seeing Sandy slip and struggle so much, that in order to make things easier for her I took all of our bathroom rugs with a non-slip rubber backing and laid them on those floors to give her traction and a cushion. I bought as many rugs as I could find in the nearby bath store and I bought a bunch of runners from the hardware store, spending so much time there, that pretty soon everybody knew my name. Then I made a "yellow brick road" path for Sandy, from the smaller guest bedroom where she was recovering, through the kitchen-den and unto the backyard patio to the grass, and blocked other areas of the house with baby gates. Our home was beginning to look like a gypsy encampment with all the mismatched multi color mats, but I would do anything to make Sandy feel safe and secure. I was not about to cover our beautiful floors with wall-to-wall carpeting and figured the mats could easily be rolled up and stored in the garage if we ever had company again. The rugs proved to be enormously helpful in preventing additional injuries. I was planning on doing the same throughout the house, once the restrictions on keeping Sandy confined to a small area are lifted. After all we bought this one story house just for Sandy and want her to reclaim all the areas of her home for her use and to get her life back as normal as possible.

About a week after her leg surgery, the surgical vet called to see how Sandy was doing and said that the results of her biopsy were positive and that Sandy had sarcoma cancer, which explained the very unusual bone fracture. I was in complete shock and could not digest and process the sudden and overwhelming information that he was giving me, as that was the last thing that I ever expected him to say.

In a daze, I screamed over to Fred with the bad news and we were both completely devastated. That very same morning the doctor sent a vet technician over to pick Sandy up for more x-rays and ultrasounds to reveal if the cancer had spread to other areas. As we anxiously waited in the lobby for the results, we were told the cancer was not readily visible in the heart or lungs, but would be hard to tell if the cancer was in the blood vessels because it would be microscopic. That type of cancer is called hemangiosarcoma and is believed to be the most aggressive and the very worst kind possible. In most cases it starts in the spleen, which was not the case with Sandy, and is not discovered until it ruptures and sometimes is too late, because there is no test for it as there is with leukemia.

We were referred to two "state of the art" animal cancer facilities.

One in Culver City where the oncologist took more extensive x-rays and gave Sandy a morphine-like pain patch to help her along until we made our decision, and one in Ventura. The two veterinary oncologists, and an oncologist specialist surgeon as well as her three other vets, were on the same page as far as the recommended treatment was concerned. Sandy's only option would be to have her leg amputated because her leg had multiple fractures, and the tissue surrounding the bone was severely damaged and would never be able to heal, and the cancer would rapidly spread to other areas if left untreated. The added benefit of the surgery would also remove the source of pain, but that would not be enough. Sandy would also need to have chemotherapy treatment afterwards. However, because the genetic make up of Shelties and Collies is different from that of other dogs, her options in chemotherapy would be limited.

Surprisingly not one veterinarian suggested having Sandy put to sleep, even though they themselves would not be involved, and no money was to be made from her illness. Her vital signs were still good as well as her overall health. We try to do what we can to save our loved ones whether animal or human. We do it for them because we desperately want them to get well, but also especially for us, the ones who will be left behind. We hope that there might be a miraculous cure overnight and we are always willing to give it a try. Nobody seems to say let's put grandma down, even though she might be 100 years old, and spare her of her misery when there is no cure, do they? Even though humans with some forms of cancer suffer longer and their quality of life is very poor, we wait till they leave us. However, it is very common to have an animal put down, but for humans wanting relief and release from their suffering there is a stigma attached, as in the cases involving Dr. Jack Kevorkian's patients who begged for mercy and peace to no avail. I suppose that most doctors' philosophy is to help their patients to live and not to die.

Giving Sandy a little time to recover from the bone fracture surgery, the oncology vet in Ventura performed the surgery removing her right hind leg three weeks later. It was extremely traumatic for all of us to have Sandy go though all of this in addition to what she went through during the previous surgery and the very difficult recovery for the fracture. This surgery proved to be a very challenging one because the pin that was placed in the bone beforehand by the other vet, had migrated upwards and kept re-shattering the bone, further damaging the surrounding tissue and it was not clear if it contaminated other healthy tissue with cancer cells.

In addition Sandy developed aspiration pneumonia while in ICU where she had been for the past six days. She was put on a ventilator with oxygen after they heard her labored breathing and panting and gave her antibiotics in an IV as well. This proved to be lifesaving and the next day there was a vast improvement, especially in her disposition.

The oncology animal hospital is open twenty-four hours a day, seven days a week with a full staff of vets and techs and I was very pleased at the way they monitor their patients staying at the facility. There were actually more doctors there than there are in hospitals for humans during the middle of the night.

It is a half hour away from our home and Fred and I made the drive twice daily to visit and feed Sandy. My Mom and Randy would drive forty-five minutes to sometimes an hour in traffic, just to see her and to show their support. I would bring Sandy her special home cooked food and made sure she knew that we loved her and had not abandoned her.

It has all been a tremendous financial burden on us. Fred has been paying 100% of our bills because I had not worked for a long time after my aneurysm, and have again taken time off to care for Sandy since her fracture. I have maxed out my credit cards and gone through most of my savings and fortunately my mom has given us financial support to cover a part of the expense of Sandy's treatment. My pet insurance only covered a miniscule portion and has now permanently excluded Sandy from further coverage.

But I was willing to do anything to save Sandy as long as she was not suffering and the pain could be controlled until her recovery, and her chances of survival and having a quality of life that she deserved were good.

Even though I have always taken a great deal of pride in the fact that I have an excellent A-Plus credit score, I was willing to go bankrupt for Sandy if necessary. That is how much I adore her.

Throughout this entire ordeal Sandy has been "a brave little soldier" as I often tell her. Just the fact that Sandy was able to survive the horrible bone fracture, two very major surgeries and pneumonia in such close proximity as well as all the anesthesia, antibiotics, pain killers and other drugs at her age, is close to miraculous and a testament to her hardiness, spirit and nobility.

We never leave her side and Fred and I take turns going out and my Mom or Randy comes to help us out whenever possible just to give us a break because we are both overwhelmed. Without the support of my family we would not have managed. If over the years we would only leave Sandy alone for a few hours at a time when she was healthy, from now on she will never be left alone, not even for a minute, for the rest of her life.

As Sandy is recovering from her leg removal, she is as spirited as ever, proud and fierce and stoic. Sandy is of strong and sturdy Scottish stock and she is a magnificent creature with a very regal demeanor. I can picture her atop a windswept bluff, overlooking the rocky ocean in the harsh climate of the Scottish Highlands, wearing a plaid cape and a beret and carrying a walking stick while proclaiming, "I Shetland Sheepdog am a survivor and I rule my kingdom."

I decided it would be a lot easier this time around to just have Sandy recover in our master bedroom because of the double French doors leading directly to the garden. I moved her bolster bed back into our bedroom but turned it around, so that she would be facing the yard, making it easier for Sandy to get up and go straight out without having to turn around and lose her balance.

Even though I would keep the doors open most of the time so Sandy could see outside and get some fresh air, I would block off the door with a baby gate so that if I left the room for one second she wouldn't be running loose in our backyard and possibly injuring herself. I also blocked off the room with more baby gates so she could still be confined, giving Sandy a chance to rest and heal; yet giving her enough space to comfortably move around.

The only problem with the new set up was that there was a four-inch step down from the French doors to the uneven stone patio below. I had to somehow build a little padded ramp, so that Sandy would not lose her footing and trip, and injure herself on the hard surface. Once again I was at the hardware store looking for a large piece of plywood that would cover the patio. They had to cut it up for me because I would not be able to get it inside my car, and I would have to unite it with a thick outdoor tape once I came home. I then got a very large sheet of 1-inch thick Styrofoam typically used as insulation, to pad the wood and finally covered it up with the runners for traction. That way if Sandy fell again, she would have a cushion.

It made our hearts ache also seeing Sandy trip on the metal piece at the bottom of the French doors, which we had not anticipated as happening. So I covered it with a thick yoga mat that I cut up for padding, so if she fell at the doorway she wouldn't hurt herself, then re-covered it with a smaller bath mat. It was all a work in progress that needed to function for her safety.

It completely surprised me at how well Sandy was adjusting and managing on three legs, especially with the protective soft-cone-collar resembling a morning glory flower that they put around her neck, so she won't chew on her incisions, giving them time to heal. All the oncologist veterinarians predicted that Sandy would do better once the source of pain is removed, and that even dogs with three legs are very resilient. At the moment Sandy shows no signs of slowing down, sometimes showing off as if to say to us "look what I can do", and spends a lot of time hopping around our home and backyard like a little grasshopper.

However, Sandy's attitude changed drastically once the stitches were removed and the cone came off. For the longest time I could not figure out why she had done so much better before, with the protective collar on, even though she had less of a peripheral view. I suspect that what you can't see won't hurt you; much like a horse with blinders.

I was worried sick about the traumatic effect it would have upon Sandy once she realized she no longer had her leg. But she put up a brave front in true sheepdog fashion never letting on that it bothered her. The vets had reassured us that Sandy would not miss her leg at all and that animals don't see themselves as handicapped, but I disagree with them all.

Nevertheless, as I had suspected, Sandy lost her self-confidence and had a huge setback. She has also become fearful of nighttime, constantly perking up her ears on alert mode, listening to every sound that we could not hear. Sandy now had a psychological block and perhaps feels that she is no longer in control of her kingdom as she once was. Now she had a disadvantage, and would not be able to react as easily and quickly in the dark, and chase or outrun all the other outdoor creatures that surface only at night if she needed to.

Sandy's habits also changed. She no longer slept on any of her beds where she used to love to curl up and rest her head on the side bolsters. Maybe because she finds it harder to get up from a soft, cushy surface without a firm support. Sandy has also stopped going potty before bedtime as she always used to do, and no amount of coaxing with treats would get her to go out to the well-lit backyard, even with me or Fred by her side. I tried to carry her out a few times and she became aggressive and stressed out, and I even tried using the sling again, but she tried to bite it. So we decided it was best to stop pressuring Sandy with our anxiety, and hoped that she would go on the potty pads next to the garden doors, just in case she needed to go in the middle of the night. But Sandy refused to use them, holding it again anywhere from 12-18 hours on average till the next day, just as she had done after the pin was placed on her fractured bone.

This has been driving us both crazy and we are really concerned that her kidneys will become damaged or that she will develop a urinary tract infection. We called the vet for his opinion and he feels that her needs are changing and that if she really has to go to the point where she is bursting, Sandy will make the effort to get up and pee, and that we all need to adjust.

I finally understood Sandy's fears when I heard a pack of coyotes running down the canyon one house over. It is the most eerie bone chilling sound. However, our block fences are high, and they would have to climb up into the neighbor's yard first, whose fences are even higher because they hit the street. It is frightening to think that all that time we were living with a false sense of security when I later read that coyotes can scale a wall and even climb up on to a 13-foot fence.

The problem with coyotes is that since we have been encroaching on their habitat as the human population expands, they have no other recourse than to approach the urban neighborhoods for food and are being sighted more frequently not only at dawn and dusk, when they are known to hunt, but also in broad daylight even on the flatlands. All the animal care organizations recommend not leaving any pet food or unsecured garbage outside as a preventative measure in attracting predators as well as never leaving infants, small children or pets alone without supervision.

Sandy has never been left unattended in our yard, not even in the daytime for a minute because then there are the other predators to deal with such as hawks and owls, although I have never personally seen one, and large crows who are capable of taking a small dog or cat with their claws, never to be seen again.

A Chihuahua who lived a couple of blocks down, was suddenly and tragically taken away when a large crow swooped into his yard, right in front of its shocked and helpless owner. I am now hearing more often about pets being walked on leashes in their very own back yard as a precautionary measure. That way they can be quickly pulled away from predators, giving them a better chance of survival.

A building contractor that I had met, reported that when they were remodeling a tall commercial building in the neighborhood, were perplexed to find a bunch of collars belonging to cats and dogs, on the rooftops. That story gave me the creeps and made me be even more cautious. Being careful not to open up old wounds, the diplomatic builder was nice enough to call and to notify the people with the missing pets, whose tags had phone numbers, in order to help them get closure in knowing what had happened to their pets. Most of them thought they had lost their animal companions to coyotes. All the people he reached wanted the collars back and were very appreciative.

I am sad that Sandy and I will never be able to go out on walks around the block again. Those times were "mommy and me" days. Sometimes I had to remind Sandy that she did not own the block, when she barked at any passerby.

In order to give Sandy more mobility inside our house, I had Luke, Sandy's groomer who knows how to do everything, build a wood ramp for the step down living room where Fred watches TV on the large screen. We had been blocking off that part of the house with baby gates because of the one step and we don't want Sandy to fall and injure herself. But Sandy seems determined to go down there like she used to and we don't want to deprive her of that, so we made it happen. However, the ramp angle is steep so even though she can hop down with no problem, Sandy cannot get herself back up and trips even though it is padded. That saddens and upsets us tremendously. We have given Sandy access several times, but I had to have my brother or a neighbor help me get her back up, and it stresses Sandy out because she refuses to be helped or carried and she gets very agitated.

Because of the conflicting and very confusing reports from the pathologists after Sandy's leg was removed, we were no longer convinced that we wanted to put her through chemotherapy. Some vets believed that she had hemangiosarcoma; others did not see evidence of that, partly due to the surgical hemorrhage obscuring the results. But one thing was for sure; if she did chemo it would damage her heart. My question was do the benefits of chemotherapy outweigh the damage it would do to her heart and her overall immune system? The chemo would certainly not cure her and it would take her strength away. It would maybe only help to prolong her life for a little while or perhaps even shorten it as it happens in some cases, and there would also be the discomfort of the probable side effects such as vomiting, diarrhea, appetite loss and fur loss.

Fred and I had a dilemma on our hands and very little time to make up our mind about our options, as time is of the essence, and we thought long and hard about what was best for Sandy and decided to let her just be and skip the chemotherapy. Sandy has already endured so much and because she is almost twelve and only has three legs, she exerts herself a great deal more as she is now forced to hop around instead of walking and it wears her out.

So far, Sandy is eating beautifully, her breath is as fresh as ever, better than in any human that I have ever met, not to mention that she has the most beautiful teeth, clean and white and has all of them except for two back molars that chipped and broke off many years ago while chewing on one of those premium treat filled bone shanks. She never had that treat again.

Sandy's coat is also looking better than ever. It is lush and glossy and as silken as can be. The large area where she was shaven during her two surgeries, from the leg to mid-back, is almost all grown out in such a short period of time. Presently Sandy shows no outwardly evidence of feeling ill, although it is hard to tell because she can be very stoic at times. Sandy is not vocalizing pain as she had during the fracture or when she had the pin inserted in her leg. Why would we take all that away from Sandy, by making her feel sick with nausea by giving her chemo? That would defeat the whole purpose in trying to save her. Without proper nutrition Sandy would not have the strength to survive. If at any time in the future we notice that she is suffering we will do the ethical thing.

Instead of weakening her immune system with the chemotherapy, I decided to do as much research regarding supplements that would give her a boost in addition to the ones she already takes. I have added Coenzyme Q10, which supports the cardiovascular system, and DMG Liquid, which is often used by athletes to repair muscles and tissues.

Recently I have spoken over the phone and met with several potential dog walkers who really empathized with Sandy's situation and might be able to help us out in the future, especially when it starts to rain. In the past I laid out the potty pads inside our garage and Sandy would instinctively be running towards that door, happy to stay dry from the rain, and willingly used the pads because it was not inside the house. Sandy is the cleanest little doggie that I ever met and she would be mortified of soiling inside. But again because of the step down and not having the grip or cushion of the grass we would need to set up an arrangement where the walker could come several times a day for as long as needed, pick her up and carry her out to the garage, place her on the potty pads, and carry her back in.

I found it really intriguing when one particular woman dog walker-pet sitter came over to meet Sandy, coming inside our master bedroom where she was resting at the moment. For whatever reason Sandy did not like her and without even getting up she rotated her body away from the lady towards the wall behind us, completely ignoring the woman.

Maybe Sandy smelled other dogs on her and thought she might come to take her to the vet. After the lady left early that evening Sandy refused to go pee-pee at her usual time around 6:00PM, this time making it a 24-hour gap before she went again until the next morning. Fred and I were very upset and suspect Sandy was riled-up by the "intruder." Our neighbor Michelle came over again to help us very late that night and even offered to carry Sandy out, but felt Sandy was stressed out enough, and that she would be okay till the morning. Instead Michelle gently petted her, massaged her and kissed her muzzle already knowing Sandy rarely allows this from anybody but me, and especially a non-family member, but Sandy became as relaxed as a little lamb under Michelle's calm energy, falling asleep soon after. Thank you again, Michelle.

Lately Sandy has been slowing down, sleeping more than usual, and tires easily after getting up. Sometimes she seems very distant and spaced out and I wonder if she is perhaps getting dementia or losing her hearing or if god forbid, the cancer has spread, and she is not feeling well. But then the next minute Sandy barks up a storm as she always has and seems very alert and sometimes even displays her legendary dry sense of humor.

However when Sandy hops out to the yard to potty and quickly back inside, she is completely out of breath and immediately sits down and it worries me that she is very fatigued and that it is taking a toll on her heart. But I always applaud Sandy saying "good girl" after the big effort in order to boost her confidence, and she loves the recognition, feeling proud of herself, and wags her tail non-stop. I always kiss and caress her and tell Sandy that she is precious, that Mommy and Papi love her and that I will always take care of her and that she will never be alone, and Sandy blinks her eyes acknowledging what I said. I am and have always been, so in love with this creature, she is completely irresistible and charismatic and beyond gorgeous.

Early this year I finally finished a little video that I made of Sandy. Fred had given me a video camera for one of my birthdays and I had been filming her over a period of three years. I had accumulated around two hours of footage that I learned how to edit down to just under ten minutes. I learned how to upload the music and make the final cut with some special effects in my computer class. With some help I was able to put it up on YouTube. Although it may not exactly be Fellini, it was made with a lot of heart and I am very proud of it.

Anybody interested in seeing my beloved Sandy the Sheltie in action, can go to YouTube and type in the search box: <u>sandy the sheltie wallin.</u> Her first movie is titled "The Transition Years."

Even before Sandy became ill, I have often been asked over the years, by several insensitive people who know how devoted I am to her, what will I do when my beloved Sandy is no longer on this earth and if I have ever thought of getting another dog beforehand to help with the transition so I won't feel so sad or alone when she is gone? Absolutely not!

To me that question would be comparable to asking a mother whose child is sick, if she has thought of having another baby just in case? Would a mother who has several children, not miss the one that died as much, because she still has a few more left? What an asinine question! I would never, ever, bring another dog or pet into our home while Sandy is still here. She has always been the "only one" and not used to sharing. That would be like trying to displace and replace her for a younger model and completely disrespectful to her as she lives out her twilight years. In hindsight, I don't think that question was meant to be hurtful or mean spirited, as much as it is a reflection of the society in which we live in, where everything is disposable, replaceable and interchangeable.

One can't escape sadness; no matter how many dogs or people we try to replace them with once they are gone. I know that when the time comes I will be completely devastated and go into full mourning because Sandy is an individual, unique and irreplaceable. I will be lost without her and feel that a part of me is gone and I will miss her forever.

Some day in the far distance, as I already know from past experience, my sadness would eventually be replaced by a smile, just thinking of all the happy times we spent together. And there will be an inner peace and comfort knowing that Sandy will live in my heart forever, as our childhood dog Estrellita does to this very day. Estrellita, means "Little Star" in Spanish. She was a Chihuahua-Maltese mix, and got her name when our childhood nanny said that she was a star that fell from the sky, when we were living in Guatemala.

As we all must eventually leave this earth, some day when nature takes over, Sandy will lie next to Estrellita, who is buried in the Los Angeles Pet Memorial Park in Calabasas, in the appropriately named "Angel's Corner." I would really like to believe that we would all meet again in a place called "Eternity." Every year for the past twenty or so years right before New Year's, my Mom, Brother and I have brought Estrellita a small living tree to plant in her memory, on the beautiful grounds where the sun seems to shine even when it rains. Some of those trees are fully-grown now which means the cycle of life continues.

Every now and then I run into the groundskeeper who has been there forever, and one day he said to me "see all those trees over there?" pointing to the far distance, "I planted them", he said with a great deal of pride and emotion while speaking about his "arbor children." And I replied, "Those are the most beautiful trees in the whole world." He gave me a smile as wide as the sky above.

Sandy just celebrated her twelfth birthday, four months after she was diagnosed with cancer. I don't know how much time we have together, but I'd rather not waste precious time dwelling about the inevitable and in the process lose today, while she continues to honor us with her presence. Each day with Sandy is a gift and we spend as much time right next to her as possible.

Fred is still Fred, and at this point in our lives, after sixteen years of marriage, I seriously wouldn't know what to do if he changed. I have come to expect a certain amount of high drama from him on a daily basis and he never lets me down. I will continue to humor him as I always have, with the great patience of a dutiful wife. It is surprising how some of the things that we find irritating about our loved ones, are the very same things that we also find endearing.

And as for me, these days I am learning one of the many important lessons that Sandy "The Sheltie" has taught me over the years. That is to live in the moment. I try not to think too much about the past or worry about tomorrow, there is only now for now.